PEARLS OF WISDOM

PEARLS OF WISDOM

Advice from a Dead Squirrel
Who Knows Everything

ME PEARL

with

GEORGETTE SPELVIN

APOLLO
PUBLISHERS

CONTENTS

PART ONE • GETTING TO KNOW YOU

PART TWO • PROPER POSSUM CARE

PART THREE • AND NOW FOR A CHANGE OF PACE

PART FOUR • THE SPIRITUALITY OF SQUIRREL

Part Five • Ask Pearl

This book is dedicated to the memory of Babycakes Rowe, through whom Pearl discovered the sensational nature of her Sacred Self, and to the scores of dedicated and selfless wildlife rehabilitators who take their work too seriously to want their names connected to this book.

Bless you all.

PART ONE

Getting to Know You

Georgette's Welcome

Hello and welcome to our world. What an extraordinary experience for us to have you here.

Hang in for the duration. You'll be glad you did. This book is coauthored by myself, Georgette Spelvin, and a ferociously fun and fabulous little squirrel, Pearl de Wisdom. We're used to having guests for an afternoon now and then. Sometimes they stay late. Sometimes they leave early, sometimes through the bathroom window. There's no accounting for taste.

The advantage of short visits is that you can shove what's unsightly under the bed, metaphorically speaking. With longer visits, like this book, you're going to need some of that stuff, and retrieving it can be dodgy.

Don't misunderstand, we want you here. Very much. Especially Pearl Squirrel, who has no shame and is always on the prowl for fresh blood. Don't be alarmed. That's just one of her colorful phrases.

Let me tell you about Pearl, who, for better or worse, is my muse. Early on, Pearl developed an avid interest in world events and walnuts. She cared about art, literature, history, hickory, high finance, philosophy, filberts, anthropology, paranormal psychology, and peanuts. Pearl excels in all forms of academia and macadamia.

It would be to your advantage to make nice with Pearl. When each of us passes through the veil to the other side, it's entirely possible that she's right and we pass directly to her. I hope not, but *il faut faire attention*. She's a noxious little twit and can be vindictive if not appeased. Don't be alarmed. Forewarned is forearmed, and that's what this book is all about. So, congratulations on acquiring it.

Pearl's Welcome

CONGRATULATIONS!

You have been deemed worthy to enter, explore, and be exploited in the wonderful world of ME, Pearl de Wisdom, the one and only ascended dead squirrel. You only need one. This is the world of "Preposterosity," and you'll need to remind yourself of that frequently.

I've been alternately characterized as saint, goddess, fuzzy wuzzy widdle wodent, and purveyor of the best damn snake oil on the market. Take a moment to relax and bask in gratitude. Imagine soft, soothing music playing on K-YOU radio.

The best news you'll get today, other than if your blood tests come back and you got away with your hedonistic lifestyle, is that Pearl loves you. The biggest surprise you'll get comes midway through this book when you'll discover that you love Pearl too. Such a big lovefest. Yummy, yummy, yummy.

Although for some this lovefest may be fraught with fear and loathing, dread and disgust, due to an inability to release a tired thread-bare reality and replace it with, well, *this*.

HI THERE!

Time to open your mind and broaden your beliefs. Wider. Broader. No, more. C'mon, just say yes. Yes, I know it hurts but push through. You can do it and it will be worth it. That's the ME Pearl promise.

Forget "suspension of disbelief" because, on my honor as a dead squirrel deity, everything you are about to read is true. It actually happened, or will happen, or could happen if you play your cards right. For your convenience, we sell decks of playing cards, dice, and other assorted games of "chance" (haha hahaha) at our online store. Do yourself a favor and look it up. We at ME Pearl consider gambling a sacred ritual since, before ME, all of creation was just one big crap shoot.

Did you find that indelicate? Oh, grow up!

Work with ME, people. I'm trying to lull you into a true sense of security where you feel that everything will be just fine. Like the Petrojvic Blasting Company.[1]

This is Truth as you've never known it. Nowhere else can you change so many planes and never go near an airport.

Fasten your seat belts, friends: it's going to be a bumpy read.

Caveat Emptor

FIRST OF ALL, LET IT BE UNDERSTOOD THAT PEARL DE WISDOM absolves herself of any and all responsibility for whatever may go terribly, terribly wrong as a result of following her advice. Thank you for reading and have a nice day.

Georgette's Disclaimer

GENTLE READER,

Please accept my profound apology for the avaricious nature of Pearl de Wisdom, or Pearlie Mae as she's affectionately known by almost no one. As dead squirrels go, Pearl is really swell in so many ways and I'm honored to be her channeler, minion, and scapegoat. Yes, she's

---

1 I consider "Maledetta Orangina" from their album *A History of Public Relations Dilemmae* to be holy canon.

mercenary, rapacious, and gluttonous, but honestly, who among us isn't? More importantly, she's brilliant,[2] irresistibly loveable,[3] and full of surprises.

Pearl's Disclaimer

PEEPS,

Please accept my profound apologies for the artistic and literary short-comings of Georgette Spelvin. The only reason this book is coauthored is that most readers are shockingly hard put to accord a dead squirrel the requisite respect, so it was deemed necessary to pull in my human, Georgette, as the face of the book. Sadly, her penchant for people-pleasing precludes her from being a serious writer. But here she is. Oh goodie. Hence this book is riddled with "artistic differences." Just know that whenever the narrative devolves into pablum or schmaltz, when it's inconsistent, dull, and derivative, that's Georgette catering to the hoi polloi, no offense. So, what do I, the great and glorious Goddess of the Multiverse, Ascended Squirrel, Pearl de Wisdom, want from you, my reader?

I want you to believe in ME as I do, and you could send ME some money. Humans seem to believe that "you can't take it with you." Good. Hold onto that belief. As it happens, squirrels *can* take it with us.

We love that. And the more you send to ME, the more I will love you. And that's what you want, if you have half the brains I gave you.

---

2 Quote from Pearl de Wisdom in multiple missives.

3 Ibid.

Speaking of which, did you know that squirrel brains are poisonous? It's true.

Ill-mannered gentlemen who have been so rude as to shoot and skewer us over a firepit have eaten our brains to their everlasting regret . . . .

Opinion please, take another look at this book cover. Go ahead. You must have found it sufficiently compelling to now be in possession of the book. Yes? But imagine: a picture of ME in a crown of thorns with blood dripping tastefully down the camera side of my face and the title *The Passion of the Pearl*.[4] Good, right? Why couldn't we get that past the editor?

---

4 What must it be like to live in the mind and gut of Mel Gibson?

Granted there is a smidge of appropriation involved, but it sure would have been gripping. And Jesus, who I can tell you firsthand (I conduct Religious Leader Summits over here) is a mensch, would have given an enthusiastic endorsement. He's a very supportive fellow. You'd like Him. But He tends to be single-species focused. Oh, sure He talks about birds and sheep and, our personal favorite, camels, but only as metaphors. How do you expect us to thrive and excel and prevail when reduced to metaphors?

Backstory of Pearl by Pearl

ONCE UPON A TIME, THERE WAS A WILD SQUIRREL NAMED CHCK CHK CHCK, who gave birth to ME. I was a spring baby. The first time out of the nest, wouldn't ya know, something really bad happened to one of my back legs and CHCK CHK CHCK took me to this House of Nuts she'd been frequenting for the past year and barked and barked and banged on the window until a weird witchy hermit and purveyor of said nuts came out and just scooped ME off the fence. It was shock at first sight.

Something called "bonding" happens. I don't like it. You don't like it. It's demeaning, but it happens. So, the big pale weird witchy hermit, who shall henceforth be known as Pink Mama, or PM, wrapped ME up and delivered ME to a gas mask in a bad smelling colorless building and, when I got back to the Nut House, the dangling mangled mess that had been my right rear leg was gone. GONE! **GONE!**

Quelle souffrance. Pearl knows pain. Wisdom does not come easy, my friends, fans, followers, fanciers, and financiers. Once my socket was healed, PM tried repeatedly and zealously to return ME to CHCK CHK CHCK, who still came around for the free nuts. But nope, nothin' doing. "Yours now, lady. Pass the pecans." My natural mother was not a sentimentalist.

So, PM tried repeatedly to pass ME off to other humans who cared for "special" squirrels. They tried. But no dice. I refused to thrive, by cracky. So, PM took ME back and started believing that I loved her. Haha hahaha. My unnatural mother IS a sentimentalist. She named ME Pearl. Word to the wise: don't name anything you don't want. To name it is to tame it.

PM was then forced to learn *a lot* about looking after squirrels and she got a license saying she is a professional squirrel rehabilitator. Haha hahaha. (You have to be a squirrel to get how funny that is. Without ME poor PM couldn't even find her eyelashes!) There are squirrel protective services who come around to check. I kid you not. I think of them as the ill eagles who swoop down to make sure PM is not dressing ME inappropriately.

OK, yada, yada, yada, time went by, bored, bored, bored . . . and then first love, a brief sally into the demimonde with a squirrel named Stockton DuPres, leader of the Squirrel Liberation Army of Kentucky. But alas, he turned out to be gay. Not that there's anything wrong with that.

Then came Sam. Love of my life, Sam "the Teeth" Camplese. He was an Eastern Gray with ties to Sicily and serious "family connections," if you catch my drift. Sam and I were fated to never meet on

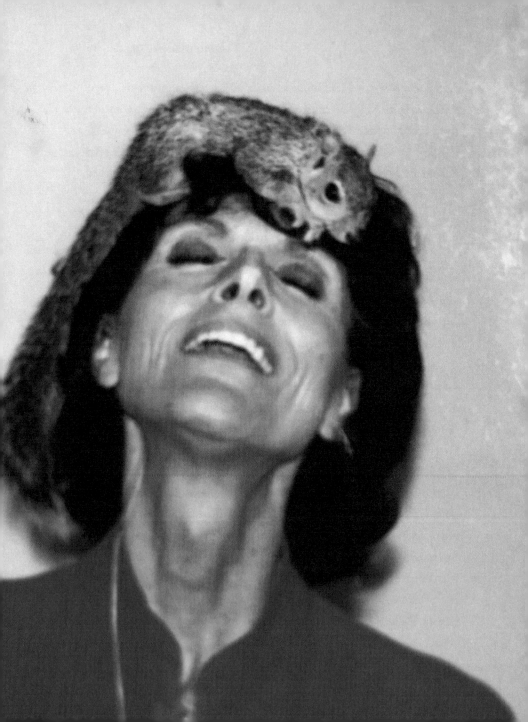

the earthly plane, although our incendiary love letters are soon to be self-published. It's different here. We met up and jumped the broom, then served it at the reception.

We spend most nights at home, gnawing Scrabble and making plans to expedite a visit from the in-laws. They don't respond to simple invitations because changing planes is "too inconvenient." They have "too much to do first," blah, blah, blah. OK, they are not ready to bite the bullet, we get it. Most humans are on the slow side. Which brings ME to the tragic predicament I now endure. Millenia ago I was sent here by ME, retroactively, to inspire all creatures and save peoplekind from your own silly selves. So, I started an advice column on my website, www.MEpearl.com. I also started a YouTube channel, MEpearlA, dedicated to the proper care of possums—somebody had to.

Although I am a natural polyglot, it wasn't enough. A prophet in her own land, etc. Seems that dead squirrels lack that certain *je ne sais quoi* required for powerful propheting. (Not so much profiting, thank ME.) So I was forced to enlist Pink Mama as my mouthpiece. *Quel dommage. Quelle douleur.* The sublime meets the ridiculous.

So far, she's the only one who can hear me. Her interpretations may be batshit crazy, but hers is an easy-access mind (something like an Easy-Bake Oven) with few obstacles and little interference. Yes, she's simple. The big pink human who was my earthly caregiver and is now my channeler is, to put it kindly, an albatross. I listen to Seth and Abraham and Ramtha complaining (yes, kindred spirits hook up over here) but HA! their challenge is nothing compared to . . . well, don't get ME started. Georgette is no Yelena Petrovna Blavatsky, that's all I can say.

Just know that I am accepting applications for a new and far worthier channeler. So, if you have been awakened at three in the morning by what sounds like squirrel chatter in your head, you may be the second coming and the next anointed by ME, the great and powerful Pearl de Sagesse de Sabaduria de Wisdom de Tout.

Feel free to share personal information knowing that I, ME, Pearl, take your privacy with a grain of salt. You are permitted, encouraged even, to send money and gifts to ME through our friendly publishers at Apollo or my Patreon page. The merit of your job application will hinge on the measure of your love-offering . . . . Capitalism, kiddos.

In a nutshell, Give ME Stuff.

"Selfless giving stimulates the pleasure center of your brain."

—*Time* magazine, August 16, 2010

"I am certain beyond any reasonable expectation that giving to ME of Wisdom will change the lives of all and the course of history."

—Pearl de Wisdom, Apollo Publishers, Now

For your convenience I am including a "wish list." Better to think of it as an "I seriously want this" list. Fear not, and always remember that Pearl Loves You, and She Knows Where You Live. (I said she was full of surprises!) I am vegan, of course, so no animal products. I love rabbit-lined knickers as much as the next squirrel, but there is a greater good to consider. Actually, I AM the greater good, so no animal products, *capisce*? Yes, I am Goddess of the Multiverse, and, as such, can have anything I want, but it just gives ME a little buzz and tingle to get gifts or—to be real—tribute. So pony up, puppies.

a. Walnuts

b. You choose

c. Almonds

d. Universal veterinary care

e. Pecans

f. You choose

g. Hazelnuts

h. Climate change reversal
   (I could do it, myself, but
   I'm curious to see just how
   long you'll let this go.)

i. Pistachios (although
   I weary of the
   labor-intensity)

j. You choose

k. Peanuts—*not!* First of all, peanuts are legumes, not nuts. More importantly, they have little nutritional value and often contain toxic mold. If you *must* feed peanuts to someone, save them for the elephants when you go on safari, and even then be prudent. Other non-nuts to avoid include cashews, due to high oxalate content. I could go on and on, but that would just make you lazy. Look it up!

Backstory of Pearl by Georgette

PEARL IS A SQUIRREL, A WESTERN FOX SQUIRREL TO BE PRECISE. A three-legged Western Fox squirrel to be more precise. A narcissistic three-legged Western Fox squirrel who believes she controls this planet and everything in it, to be most precise. Oh, and she's dead.

Despite that, she's here with us now. Omniscient, omnipotent, and omnipresent. That extra twenty-one grams you feel on your left shoulder? Pearl.

Over the years people have confused me, the person, with Pearl, the squirrel. They're way off. I'm just someone who prefers to remain anonymous because, honestly, I find this whole thing quite embarrassing. The squirrel makes me do it. Really. She channels herself through me. The opossums and I are merely pawns in the paws of this egomaniacal, driven, yet often charming and profound little squirrel, who lived and died and then came back . . . with an agenda! And, yes, against my will and better judgment, I am here to serve that agenda.

Here's a semi-secret. I, Georgette Spelvin, am actually Pink Mama. At seven weeks old, Baby CHK, a.k.a. Pearl de Wisdom, fell into my care after a terrible accident requiring her right rear leg to be amputated. This made her a non-releasable, a label distinguishing wildlife who are unable to successfully fend for themselves in the wild.

And so I rearranged my life to accommodate her special needs. She blossomed and thrived and grew into a personality I could have never predicted. And then it happened; I fell in love with her *à la folie*.

Over time, Pearl did what many dependent disabled creatures

do; she became dictatorial. Her favorite subject was, and remains, herself. That's why she capitalizes her favorite word, ME. ME Pearl Productions produces a plethora, 147 and counting, of YouTube videos on our channel MEpearlA. MEpearl.com is our website where you can give Pearl money, have your deepest life questions answered, and give Pearl more money.

You won't be insulted by getting anything in return, no silly certificates or tacky T-shirts.

Instead, you'll be honored with the truth. TRUTH, as Pearl sees it.

Plus, you receive the added reward of knowing that your love-offering made a dead squirrel just a little bit happier, and who wouldn't want that? Later in this book we'll give you examples of Pearl's life-altering advice from the heart and mind and only Pearl knows what else may be operating within her. Perhaps your most salient concern has already been expressed and satisfied.[5]

"What I Did for Love": A Spelvinian Sonnet for Pearl by Georgette

What fickle tricks of Goddesses

Propelled Thee from the liquid amber tree

And with what cries unearthly did Thy mother call to me

To let me know of Thine infirmity

With mine own sleepy eyes

I did so mournfully behold

A torn appendage hanging loose

So cold, misshapen and refusing use

For such a trusting infant I did reach

And did beseech Thee, "Let me comfort Thee"

And hie Thee to a faithful nurse, who wouldst with pure intention

And with knife, amputate this wicked curse

---

5 See Part 5: Ask Pearl.

And spare Thy blessed life,

Relieve Thee of thine misery

And let Thine legs add up to three.

And thus Thou was entrusted to my willing outstretched hand

And now my home, my heart, my land, my everything
belongs to Thee.

Oh, Spoiled Rodent,

How quickly didst Thou wrap me round thy furry fluffed tail

And chatter falsities of tenderness, and all the while

Thee left a trail of wreckage close behind.

A dozen seasons now have come and gone

And still I thrill to Thee

My home's become *ménage à neuf*

Oh woof, woof, woof, the others vainly call

For all would cherish basking in the countenance

I save for Thee alone.

Dear one, it was with joy and ecstasy

I brought the forest unto Thee.

An apple tree brings thrice the happiness

Of any other fruit or foliage.

My muse, take pity on my dearth of creativity

Unearth the mystic sensitivity, the certainty

With which I first touched Thee.

I held a jewel in my hand

A precious trembling Pearl,

And that became thy name, my pet

And never once have I regretted loving Thee.

For sooth, one truth I see

This wretched world became a sacred place

When I didst first behold the face of Thee

    My darling squirrel.

Sonnet Critique by Pearl de Wisdom

MY PINK MAMA/GEORGETTE loves ME SO MUCH. CLEARLY, she's no poet, but the kid's got heart.

The Problem with Possums by Pearl

SO, IN ORDER TO LOOK AFTER ME PROPERLY, AND LEGALLY, Georgette had to get licensed by the Department of Fish and Game, now called the Department of Fish and Wildlife due to a particularly effective hissy fit thrown by yours truly. "Look, chums," says I in squirrel, "I am neither fish nor game. And just what do you mean by 'game,' anyway? Seems a pretty loaded and mean-spirited game. And nobody wins. One 'player' is maimed or murdered and the other player's soul withers and goes straight to hell." But I digress.

I think Gretch—that's Gretchen Wyler—put it best when she said, "I look forward to the day when animals will have the right to run if they have legs, swim if they have fins, and fly if they have wings."

In the olden days Georgette worked with Gretch on the Genesis Awards, given annually to individuals in the major news and entertainment media for producing outstanding works that raise public awareness of animal issues.

Since Gretch[6] passed through the veil and came to join ME on this side, the Genesis Awards have been sponsored by the Humane Society of the United States.

To get licensed, Georgette had to be trained in the care and rehabilitation of a whole *mishegoss* of "small mammal" wildlife. The next thing you know we are up to our tails in opossums. I jest not. Technically, that would be a passel o' possums.

Remember the early *Star Trek* episode "The Trouble with Tribbles"? Well, it's a lot like that. And camels. Once they get their nose under your tent, as sure as oaks from little acorns grow, the rest will follow. Take it from ME, opossums are pathetic. For example:

---

6 The only one allowed to call her Gretch is ME. Don't even think about it.

LET'S EVALUATE THE EFFECTIVENESS OF THE OPOSSUM'S DEFENSE SYSTEM

SPOILER ALERT, ît's BAD. REALLY, REALLY BAD.

1. Possum crossing the road sees and hears and feels oncoming vehicle

2. Possum's full arsenal of defense mechanisms engage

3. Possum plays dead

4. Possum is dead.

How far could Jack London get with that?

WHAT'S NOT PARTICULARLY IMPORTANT TO KNOW ABOUT (O)POSSUMS

HO HUM BUT YOU WANT TO KNOW AND PEARL IS NOTHING IF NOT generous to a fault.

This is a possum from Australia:

and an opossum from North America:

Some folks pronounce the "o" and some do not. Either way you say it, people who care (can you imagine?) will quibble and squabble and grow contentious until you are perfectly justified in biting them.

(O)possums are marsupials, which means they have pretty little pouches that can accommodate thirteen babies who start out the size of rice grains. They develop in the pouch for a couple of months and then climb up on mama's back to see the world for themselves. I could tell you about the male's bifurcated penis but I don't want to.

Within three and a half years (o)possums drop dead, which could seem sad if death weren't a portal into more magnificence than you can possibly imagine.

Here's the thing. I'm gonna call 'em whatever I feel like in the moment, like I do everything. Just know, if you care, that all the marsupials coming through our gates and fences are Virginia opossums.

So, how did we get started with our Possums on Parade video series? Just a fluke.

You may remember Maryjean Ballner, the cat massage lady. Her video "Your Cat Wants a Massage" exploded all over YouTube sometime in 2009. When Georgette saw this, her mind naturally galumphed to wildlife. Since Georgette is also a professionally trained and certified masseuse through the Institute of Psycho-Structural Balancing, adapting the techniques to possums was a snap. After that, we acquired a camcorder, created a YouTube channel, and bingo bobster, Bob's your lobster! In 2010 we posted our first video, and the fan mail began to pour in.

PART TWO

Proper Possum Care

Proper Opossum Massage

FOLLOWING ARE INSTRUCTIONS ON PROPERLY MASSAGING YOUR possum.

If you've been concerned about your opossum's flexibility and structural well-being, it's time to learn about proper opossum massage.

If you have a senior opossum it's possible that she or he has lost some of the elasticity and spring some opossums are known for. That's why, along with regular massage, it's important to give a daily supplement of glucosamine chondroitin with MSM. Proper opossum nutrition is of utmost importance and will be covered in another section.

Before continuing with the massage instructions, let me address the elephant in the room: the vast majority of opossums belong outside. If you see one there, leave it there. If you come across an ill, injured, or orphaned opossum, contact a professional wildlife rehabilitator immediately. Now would be a good time to look up this information and enter it into your smartphone.

If, after all this, you are still left with an opossum, well, stretch that animal out on a table and give him or her a massage. If you don't have a proper massage table you can purchase one at a marsupial supply outlet, or you can simply use an ironing board. Be sure to have a soft fleecy cover so as not to snag one of the delicate little toenails.

Begin by moisturizing your hands with an unscented lotion. This is because you may have a possum with a sensitivity to environmental allergens.

Now lift your arms and hands above your head and shake. Shake vigorously. Shake out the stress. Harder! More! Shake it all out! Take a deep breath and stretch. Reach for the ceiling. And release.

Ragdoll and hang, letting all the remaining stress drain from your body. Now, slowly come back up to a standing position and check to see if the opossum is still on the table. If not, find your opossum and place her in the massage starting position.

Beginning at the base of the skull use your thumbs to work in slow, gentle, concentric circles. Then stretch out the trapezius, using your weight as leverage. Push and fan using all of your fingers.

Push and fan. Repeat three times. Now work down the spine with both hands briskly stimulating each and every vertebra as you go. At this point the opossum should shake all over with the release of its own stress.

Move to the side of the opossum, placing your outstretched hands on the rib cage, and pull up. Oh, but that should feel good. Move to the other side and repeat. Always work both sides of the body. Otherwise you might inadvertently interfere with your opossum's natural chi, and nobody wants that.

Next you're going to knead down the quadriceps, looking for knots. When you find one, continue kneading gently but firmly until the knot is dissolved. Here's where patience really pays off. Do the same on the other side. If there are many knots, this procedure could take several hours, but rest assured that it is time well spent.

Everybody loves a good foot massage, and the opossum is no exception. So dab a suitable unguent on your fingertips and find the shiatsu pressure points on the pads of the feet. Press gently and awaken all those little nerve endings.

Now we come to the part of the massage that many people think is a whole lot of fun: the tail rub. Opossum tails can become irritated, dry, and scratchy, and we don't want that. So, using a high-end personal lubricant, you are going to lubricate the tail from the base to the tip, from the base to the tip, in slow, steady strokes.

Continue until both you and the possum feel satisfied.

One mistake that people often make when massaging an opossum is to throw off the energy. Don't do that. If you feel toxic energy release into your hands from the opossum it is up to you, as healer, to transform that energy by opening your spiritual channels and then returning that transformed energy into the opossum. Always mold your hands to the shape of the body.

When it comes time to turn your opossum over, it may be helpful to use a specially designed pillow of marsupial memory foam. Just slide the opossum gently onto its back and rest the body into the pillow. It's often helpful to have straps and duct tape handy.

Begin by working out the growing tension in the back of the neck. If hissing occurs, steer clear of the mouth while moving down to open up the pectorals.

In the event that your opossum does not wish to remain on its back, that's all right, because the next moves can be done dorsally. Reach under the opossum with both hands and begin rotating the abdomen in alternate directions in a move known as "sun moon." The right hand circles clockwise while the left rotates widdershins. As you perform this action, quietly coo or sing, "Sun moon, sun moon, sun moon, sun moon" . . . this not only aids digestion but it eases elimination as well. And we all know how important it is to keep regular.

End the massage with an invigorating all over body pat down, then reconnect the polarities, north to south and east to west. Don't mess up here or your opossum won't know if it's coming or going, and nobody wants that. Now it's time to realign the chakras. Again, accuracy is key. Begin by touching the top of the head and working down; 7, 6, 5, 4, 3, 2, and the all-important 1, or root chakra.

Lastly, you are going to sweep out the aura using your hands as little brooms. Position your hands about three inches out from the body and begin sweeping away all of the loosened toxic psychic debris. Do not be distressed if you see images, colors, or demons. It's all part of the process.

Subtle improvements can be detected almost immediately if you know what to look for. Repeat the procedure three to four times per week for best results.

Good luck. It gets better, sometimes.

Surviving Squirrel Massage

ONCE YOU ARE PROFICIENT IN PROPER OPOSSUM MASSAGE, YOU are ready to ratchet up your game and learn the secrets of surviving squirrel massage.

As you can imagine, the life of a squirrel is very stressful. The weather alone, and all that climbing and jumping, commandeering bird feeders and tormenting canines, can result in muscular tension and structural misalignment. That's where you, as compassionate healer, come in.

First, go out and catch a squirrel. Use whatever means you find convenient. It won't matter which squirrel, as they'll all react about the same.

The massage area should have warm peanut oil, soothing music other than "Muskrat Love" or songs by Alvin and the Chipmunks, and a well-stocked first aid kit, along with some other items, which, hopefully, will not become necessary.

First, stretch the squirrel out on a flat soft surface using a small, firm pillow to support the delicate cervical vertebrae and upper lumbar region.

Squirrels have razor-sharp little claws which can prove daunting to even the most seasoned practitioner. That's why I recommend keeping a pair of heavy-duty steel-reinforced iron weave feather touch massage gloves close at hand.

It's so important to gain the trust and confidence of your subject and this can be easily accomplished through simple breathing techniques.

Take a moment to align your breathing with the squirrel's breathing. Doing this over an extended period will result in your cardiac arrest, so be prudent. *In with acceptance, out with resistance. In with acceptance, out with resistance.*

If your subject remains fidgety, wrap them snuggly with a warm massage towel. Failing that, you may need a little extra support to position the body properly. Try duct tape. There's little that can't be accomplished with duct tape, rubber bands, glue, dental floss, three nails, and a sponge.

Move from the latissimus dorsi down each side of the vertebral column ending at the gluteus maximus, and press.

Always pull your thumbs, never push, especially with deep tissue work. It may be tempting, but over time you'll regret it.

If your squirrel shows signs of expiring on the table, it's better to end the massage early. Sweep out the aura and release them to process the experience. Allow them their space.

In this way, you can be sure that when the time is right, they will come scampering back for more.

Proper Possum Pedicure

I CAN'T STRESS THIS ENOUGH: THE FEET ARE THE FOUNDATION OF *the opossum.* Wouldn't this make a dandy verse for a cross-stitch pillow? Every precious little pad is important, every toe, every nail.

No matter how early you begin proper possum foot care, a life fully lived is going to show on the feet, as well as the hoary face. Please note that's H-O-A-R-Y. I would never make a moral judgment on an opossum, and neither should you.

You'll want to begin by checking over each foot, looking for broken or overgrown nails; also for cuts, calluses, fungus, and any glue residue from previous pedicures. Do not put false fingernails on an opossum. I cannot emphasize this enough. No. Just no! Especially on seniors who may be losing their grip, and I mean this literally, although you can decide what applies in your particular case.

Now, you'll need a shallow pan of warm water into which you'll measure out two tablespoons of Epsom salts. Accurate measurement is essential to a successful outcome. You may wish to add a titch of monkfish oil if your possum is into aromatherapy. Swish the salts and water all around, then lift your opossum and gingerly place her into the mixture. Several responses are possible including the urgent evacuation of pee and poop, in which case you'll have to start all over again. That's why it pays to keep plentiful possum supplies on hand, supplies such as what you'd find in any marsupial supply outlet.

Next, you're going to dry off each sweet foot, making sure to get between all the little toes. And here's a tip; all opossums love the piggy game, so play it with them often. This little piggy went to market (squeeze toe), this little piggy stayed home (squeeze toe), this little piggy had three-bean salad (squeeze toe), this little piggy had none (squeeze toe), and this little piggy (get ready for big finish) went *wee, wee, wee, wee, wee,* all the way home! Really throw yourself into the finale. With sufficient enthusiasm, this could lead to an additional evacuation. Inconvenient, but so worth the fun.

Many people use their own toenail clippers for snipping off the excess skin around the nails. With the scratchy side of an emery board, smooth off the rough edges, then, with the smooth side, *buff, buff, buff.* If you find that your opossum gets restless during this procedure, give 'em a grape.

With an orange stick, gently push back the cuticles and get ready for the really fun part of the pedicure: picking out the perfect polish. So much depends on the personality of the possum, don't you think? If you feel hot pink or neon blue is appropriate, well, all right, and I know many of you are partial to the French tip, but I prefer the more natural shades when it comes to wildlife. My personal favorites are Moss Green, Arizona Sunset, and Lady Bugs Lounging on a Lotus Blossom.

I know what you're thinking: What if the possum in question is a nail biter? Not to worry.

These polishes, along with every product from the marsupial supply outlet, are all hypoallergenic and have never been tested on animals other than this one. Never buy products that have been tested on animals. Don't do it. Karma gonna come getchu if you do. After the pedicure is complete, you may wish to consider wee booties, especially if your possum traverses rough terrain. Wouldn't want to chip a nail, would you?

Et voilà! Your possum is now fit for foot modeling, should that be the future they envision.

Proper Possum Dental Hygiene

TIME TO FOCUS ON YOUR POSSUM'S fifty razor-sharp little teeth. Be sure to stock up on chicken-flavored toothpaste if you haven't already. Now take your soft-bristled marsupial brush, being careful not to confuse it with the larger hard-bristled brush designed for equine and bovine use, and slather it with paste. Set that aside and begin your possum's oral examination by testing the articulation of the mandible. This is where you may get bit, just FYI.

You'd be surprised how many possums would benefit from good orthodontic care, but good luck getting them to keep in their retainers. Been there, done that.

If your possum is over two years old, the teeth will be sufficiently worn down that you'll no longer be in danger of losing a hand when performing this vital function.

Begin brushing in downward strokes over the incisors and the bicuspids, and then you'll want to go back to the molars, being careful not to graze the delicate soft palate. You'd be surprised how much the possums come to enjoy this procedure.

I don't recommend using your own toothbrush on the opossum as the bristles may be too firm for their sensitive gums. Contrary to what you may have heard, opossums are susceptible to gingivitis. It shows up as puffy red gums. You don't want that.

On the other paw, paler white gums may indicate that you need to boost the iron content of their food supply. Close monitoring of opossum gums does pay off.

Avoid sugary snack foods, such as caramelized maggots. This just invites Mr. Tooth Decay, tartar, and plaque. And don't fool yourself, plaque on possums is no laughing matter. No dental hygiene routine is complete without a rigorous flossing. Remember, it pays to be thorough.

And now it's time to enjoy your opossum's fresh clean breath.

Place your nose just above the back of the possum's tongue and inhale deeply. Allow that sweet possum essence to fill your every cell. *Ahh.*

When cleaning is complete, you'll want to reward your opossum, and yourself, with a complex carbohydrate. Or spaghetti is good.

Gourmet Cooking

MANY PEOPLE LIKE YOURSELF HAVE EXPRESSED AN AVID INTEREST in proper opossum gourmet cooking, when simple nutrition just isn't enough.

The opossum has an eclectic palate. They enjoy sardines, eggs, rats, yogurt, assorted meats, cheeses, sushi, organic produce, nuts, grains, and caviar, which you can save for special occasions, such as New Year's Eve or, our favorite, Groundhog Day.

For this purpose, let's consider a simple yet elegant three-course meal beginning with a crème de clam soup, sprinkled with a medley of preselected possum-friendly fine herbs and spices ground to perfection. These, like most of our ingredients, can be found in the gourmet grocery section of your local marsupial supply outlet. Why not take out a membership today?

The next course would be a seasonal fresh fruit salad consisting of kiwi, grapes, mandarin oranges, cherimoya, jackfruit, loquat, pineapple, and rhubarb. Arrange in an appetizing display and drizzle with almond yogurt. Top off with a sprig of mint. So much is in the presentation, isn't it? Yum, yum! Bet the whole family will want in on this meal.

And, once you've got them seated, it's time to spring on the greens. Let's face it, nobody likes greens unless they are soaked and floating in a stroke-promoting roux. Still, eating vegetables is de rigueur and you gotta do it. So, what we do, and you can too, is lightly steam a selection of baby carrots, pea pods, and broccoli rapini. Then we add just a pinch of trace minerals and a drop of vitamin E. Put this in the blender with a can of sardines[7] and presto! You've solved the possum produce problem. Don't go premixed to save time. It won't. Picking out all those tiny pieces of pepper and onion by hand is time consuming and labor intensive and you'll regret it.

You always want to taste test your possum's food to make sure it's not too hot or cold, too spicy or bland, or just plain revolting.

Some gourmands prefer to follow this with chopped liver, although we at ME Pearl do not. If you find liver pâté a menu-must, use chicken liver, never goose. It's not good for the chicken but it's horrendous for the goose. Spread the mixture generously on a whole grain cracker. Add an accent of parsley and bingo bango, Bob's your mango. Any of this makes for a great midnight snack. The remaining leftovers you can pack, label, and freeze in individual portions for those nights when, let's face it, you are just too tired to cook. Your opossum understands.

Now for the pièce de résistance, a nice fat rat! We want you to put on your cloak of compassion and look at this image not as potential possum food, but as a creature crying out for empathy and under-standing. Yes.

I know what you're thinking: *That rat is a prime candidate for cardiovascular exercise*. You're right.

---

7   Remove can before starting blender.

Let's get really serious for a moment. The problem of obesity in this country extends beyond our children, all the way to our rats. Attention must be paid. That's why, in subsequent books, we'll be featuring low-calorie recipes for your rat, therapeutic massage for your rat, and proper dental hygiene for your rat.

Until then, bon appétit.

While I, Georgette Spelvin, have elected to be vegan, I do not impose that on my animals. Others do and make an excellent case for doing so. For the record, our ten-year-old German shepherd has been eating V-dog vegan dog food exclusively for the past ten years and has done beautifully throughout.[8] Regular blood and urine panels have revealed healthy levels on all counts. However, the cat and possums and other wildlife passing through are served animal products. Perhaps that makes me a bad person. It is something I anguish over continually, but that's a topic for another chapter in a different book.

---

8 We receive no compensation for this endorsement.

Proper Opossum Analysis, or How to Safeguard Your Possum's Sanity, Part *Un*

ARE YOU CONCERNED ABOUT THE MENTAL HEALTH OF YOUR OPOSsum? Well, you should be. It's not the natural state for possums to be in captivity, and unless carefully and properly monitored this can lead to neurosis or even psychosis, and nobody wants a psychotic opossum.

We suggest you begin by testing for the seven major symptoms of opossum depression.

Go get your possum and follow along.

If you have a senior possum, over two-and-a-half years old, this can be a little tricky. With seniors of any species, what may look like depression can often simply be deep reverie.

Symptom #1: LOSS OF APPETITE

Get a fresh, well-washed, raw club of broccoli and set it before your possum. Was it consumed with enthusiasm or simply ignored? If ignored, do not fret. Broccoli is not an accurate indicator of appetite. I was just having a bit of fun with you. Instead, give her a grape.

Symptom #2: ANXIETY

Does your opossum jump at little noises? Whistling tea kettles? Dancing wind chimes? The popping of Bubble Wrap? (We all jump at Bubble Wrap.) How about big noises like an Amber Alert followed by police sirens and a megaphone roaring, "Pull over!" If any of these cause you or your possum to jump you may be suffering from anxiety, or a lapse in judgment.

SYMPTOM #3: LOSS OF A SENSE OF HUMOR

Many people don't know this, but the well-adjusted opossum has a great sense of humor. It's subtle, but it's there. They love a good joke. They may not understand the words but they get it vibrationally. Try this one. It rarely fails.

> This opossum walks into a bar with a duck on its head. The bartender looks up and asks "What are you doing with that big rat?" Possum replies, "That's not a rat it's a duck." And the bartender says . . . wait for it . . . "I was talking to the duck!"

We love a good joke.

If your possum seems unresponsive, it may be misleading. Check around the belly for staccato breathing and other signs of mounting mirth like spritzing liquid from the mouth and nose.

Much like people, possums respond positively to color unless they are suffering from . . .

Symptom #4: MORBIDITY

Fill your possum's environment with bright happy colors and see how quickly they cheer up, or don't.

Symptom #5: FEELINGS OF GUILT AND WORTHLESSNESS

This is bad. Don't make it worse by lying to your possum. You think they don't know. They know. For example: you're suiting up for the office, you pack your briefcase, and on the way out the door you say, "I'll be right back." No, you won't. They know that. Or, you closely examine your possum's tail and say, "No, your tail's not fat." The possum is not stupid. She knows when she has a fat tail! Have you ever placed an opossum in front of a mirror? Try it. It's interesting. They are unusually vain little creatures.

Symptom #6: LOSS OF CONCENTRATION

Help your opossum to refocus by engaging it in fun, stimulating inter-active activities. Visit your local marsupial supply outlet and check out the wide variety of enrichment toys, like birdy bling on a string. Here's one you can make yourself.

Take an old piece of jewelry, like your wedding ring. Superglue it to the end of a broom handle. Lightly steam several strands of spaghetti. You can add food coloring for an extra touch of pizzazz. Thread the flaccid strands of spaghetti through the wedding ring and secure by tying the ends. You are now ready to dangle . . . and jerk! Dangle . . . and jerk! This toy is sure to catch the attention of even the most blasé opossum.

Or, remove the rod from the window blind. It will be more labor intensive adjusting the light but, well, it's a trade-off. Now go into one of your "everything" drawers and pick out some old "something" under a pound. Attach with elastic which can be removed from several pieces of high-end ladies' undergarments. Again, dangle . . . and jerk! Dangle . . . and jerk! This entire distraction device, much like life really, is held together by rubber bands and superglue. Or you can try the ever popular laser light on the wall. That's an occasional winner, I'm told.

Still need to ratchet things up? Enter the world of feng shui. Redecorate your possum's habitat. Change the color scheme. Rearrange the furniture. Replace the looking glass with a fun house mirror.

How can you stay depressed when you're scrambling to get your bearings? So many tricks, and folks, I got a million of 'em. Lastly,

Symptom # 7: AGGRESSION

Most opossums will not bite unless you stick your hand in their mouth. And even then it's not certain (which you must believe in order to undertake proper possum dental hygiene with the necessary confidence). But don't be arbitrary.

Pop Quiz

You're walking along, la-la-la, when you spot a possum on a fence at dusk. You,

A. Contact a professional wildlife rehabilitator and say, "I just saw an opossum. Do *something*!" You might be surprised how often that happens.

B. Approach the animal and stick your hand in its mouth to see if it will bite.

C. Say, "Hey! Wassup, Possie?" and move along.

The answer is C because, and here's one more time to drive it home, the vast majority of opossums belong outside. If you see one there, leave it there. If you come across an ill, injured, or orphaned opossum, contact a professional wildlife rehabilitator immediately.

If, after all this, you are still left with an opossum, stretch that animal out on a couch and analyze it.

Proper Possum Analysis, Part *Deux*

NOTHING IS MORE IMPORTANT THAN YOUR OPOSSUM'S MENTAL health measured by emotional stability and a positive outlook, because everybody enjoys an optimistic opossum. Every opossum is different, so the sanity standards for one may not apply to another. And that is why we often use a well-respected personality trait test and cognitive-style assessment, the Myers-Briggs Type Indicator—marsupial adaptation, of course.

This is a powerful tool in helping determine your possum's preferences, motivations, and, in some cases, value system. However, this may take days to administer and your possum may become impatient, so forget it.

You might try the trendy Enneagram Personality Test. Answer about forty questions the way you believe your opossum would answer. Be honest. Then read through a detailed analysis of each of the nine Enneagram types to determine what most accurately describes your little darling and see how well it coordinates with the questionnaire results. Here's a time-saving tip: your possum is a four.

What you can do instead, and it's perfectly all right, is fall back on the information derived from your possum's astrological sign. For example, if you know that (name) is a Gemini, her or his lightning-fast personality changes may seem just a little less pathological.

Geminis crave entertainment, so don't be shy; a little song, a little dance, a little seltzer down your pants.[9] It all goes a long way in staving

---

9   *The Mary Tyler Moore Show*, S06 E07 "Chuckles Bites the Dust."

off aberrant behavior.

Remember, the only difference between an eccentric and a psychotic is the eccentric knows who not to talk to.

Proper Possum Analysis, Part *Trois*

IS YOUR POSSUM SHOWING SIGNS OF ENNUI? IT HAS BEEN SAID that possums are susceptible to SAD, seasonal affective disorder. That means someone gets depressed by the dark—although with possums being nocturnal, that doesn't seem likely, so forget it.

They can't tell us how they feel because they don't communicate in words. They communicate in actions, such as sliming (lots of wet licking) your foot. It means, I love you, I love you, I love you! Doing this to a bicycle tire means much the same thing.

They also project mental pictures, usually of a similar nature. To see these pictures you must first clear your channels by eliminating everything extraneous from your energy field. Close your eyes and wave your hands in front of your face. Images will start flying by with the speed of the tornado scene in *The Wizard of Oz*. It will behoove you to stay grounded.

Most people totally fail to realize the opossum's yearning to belong. Don't wait for an invitation, be the first in your workplace to celebrate Bring Your Opossum to Work Day. Won't that be popular? It's sure to catch on. But what about evening, you ask. Well, be the first one in your social circle to institute Bring Your Opossum to a Gallery Opening, Cocktail Party, Movie Premiere, Speed Dating Activity, Ballroom Dancing Competition, Book Club, 12-Step Meeting, etc. You'll discover that, with few exceptions, like funerals and brises, the well-behaved opossum is welcome everywhere. And what an icebreaker!

But, and I cannot emphasize this enough, nonalcoholic beverages only. Possums tend to have a little drinking problem. They are bad drunks.

But, a sober opossum is a social asset. That bears repeating, *A sober opossum is a social asset.*

Makes a catchy cross-stitch pillow sampler.

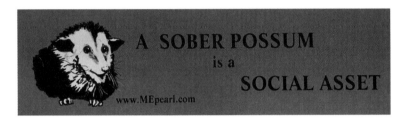

Plus, they are the fashion statement *toujours à la mode.* Don that little black dress or suit you keep for special occasions, add a splash of color and simple jewelry, then just fling that animal over your shoulder like a continental soldier, and bingo buffle, Bob's your truffle. Who says you can't wear fur? Of course, you can and should wear fur, as long as there is a happy little body indwelling.

Standards of Excellence

You know, a lot of people ask me, "Georgette, is there a standard for possum excellence?" Well, yes there is, and I'm going to share it with you now. Hundreds of prizes have been won by possums out of the ME Pearl Marsupiary. Champions and grand champions, all.

Do you think your possum could be a champion? Let's find out. Go get your possum. You're going to need a styling comb, measuring tape, magnifying glass, flashlight, pen, paper, calculator, clipboard . . . and a grape.

And now let's see if you have a champion or simply a companion; not that there's anything wrong with that.

The good news: if you have a possum, you can be pretty sure it's a purebred. *But*, is it competition material? Possum showing is an elite activity. Not for the riffraff. You know who you are; not that there's anything wrong with that. Answer the following as objectively as possible.

When you look at your possum, is what you see exquisite? That's worth fifty points. Is it swell? Thirty points. Meh? That's a zero. Sickly? Minus seventeen. Dead? That's an automatic disqualification. And why would you enter a dead possum in a competition? I mean, really!

Begin with your styling comb and lift and feather inch-long strips of fur over the entire body. Depending on personal skill and possum size this can take between one and seven hours.

Now for the feet. Feet are the foundation of the opossum. Toes should be straight, not splayed or pigeon. The proper number is five on the front feet and four on the back. Anything else is just wrong and will eliminate you, at least from the better possum shows.

Eyes should be round, clear, and open. Crossed eyes, while cute as the dickens, is a fault as it indicates that your possum is just too darn fat. There goes another fourteen points. If this is you, write it down. Possums should have a healthy appetite, and a wide variety of treats may be used in the show ring, but if your possum spits up the treat, *Ooo*, that's gonna cost you.

Now, get your flashlight. Signal for your opossum to open her or his mouth and carefully inspect the entire cavity. The tongue should be pink and supple and not pointing at anyone, because that's just rude. Teeth should be shiny, white, sharp, evenly distributed with proper occlusion, and never under any circumstances used to bite the judge because that would cost you points, which, depending on the severity of the injury, could end an otherwise promising career, at least in the United States and parts of Canada. South America, Estonia, and the United Kingdom tend to be more lenient in these matters. But, in any event, there will be a penalty of twenty-four points. If your possum has ever bitten anyone, including you, just deduct those twenty-four points right now. Why wait?

Now, get your tape measure. Ears should be round with the capacity to go flat, because that's so darn cute. Especially when eating bananas. But I digress. They should be an equal distance from each other and from the tail, ideally 2.4 and 19 inches, respectively. Any disparity will be considered a fault and will cost you points. So, deduct the number of inches you are either over or under those measurements as points and write them down.

Stacking: stacking is making sure that each body part aligns with every other body part at the proper angulation. Proper possum conformation gets too little attention these days. Don't you agree? Well, I blame the media. And when was the last time you had a lively discourse on bifurcation? I'll bet it's been awhile. Am I right? Well, that can change. It must and it will.

You'll want the accurate circumference of your possum's head, so useful when picking out hats. Here the gold standard is six inches. If the possum is six months or younger subtract one inch. If over two years and male just double everything.

And now the girth. Wrap your tape measure round and round and round, getting as much of the girth as you possibly can. You can choose to do your measurements in centimeters—three centimeters equals 1.18 inches—*but* you will then have to deduct 318 points from your final tally.

Possums really enjoy this attention, don't they? Have you noticed the incalculable amount of bonding taking place?

Attitude is a major consideration. Possums should be cheerful, thirty points; proud, forty-seven points; and curious, nineteen points; but not spunky, minus eleven. We hate spunky. They should be able to hold a single thought for over ten seconds. Otherwise, they likely have attention deficit disorder.

Get your calculator. Now, take your chart and add up the measurements, subtract the deductions, add the bonus points, and the closer you come to seventy-eight the closer you are to excellence.

Reality check: Once more, the vast majority of possums belong outside. If you see one there leave it there. If you come across an ill, injured, or orphaned opossum, contact a professional wildlife rehabilitator immediately.

End reality check. If, after all this, you are still left with an opossum, bathe it, groom it, and enter the fast-paced exhilarating world of possum competition. But, if you're clumsy or your possum simply doesn't like you, you may wish to engage a professional handler. Don't know one? Just check the bulletin board at any marsupial supply outlet.

In the unlikely event that there are no reputable possum shows in your area, get together with like-minded possum aficionados and start one, using this as your standard of excellence.

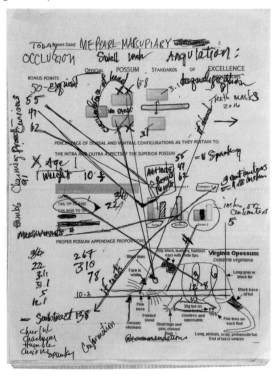

Well, I hope you've found this edifying and inspirational and that you, too, will become winners, like us. Winners winning, cause that's what winners do, we win. But don't let that intimidate you. Just have fun with it.

See you on the circuit.

Proper Opossum Poetry Corner

It takes a special possum to appreciate poetry and I'm proud to say that here, at the Spelvin Family Ranch, special possums abound. If your opossum is special, well deck that animal out in black and take it to a poetry reading or, better yet, a slam.

Over the years we at ME Pearl Enterprises have sponsored many poetry contests featuring, you guessed it, the opossum, and we'd like to share with you some of the winning entries.

I'll bet most of you have had the experience of your possum rolling her eyes at the prospect of another Native American *pourquoi* story. We suggest you start a collection of poetry for reading to your possum at bedtime. That would be about the time your morning alarm goes off.

Let's begin with this entry by Anonymous entitled "Here Opossum, There Opossum, Everywhere Opossum Possum."

Oh Possum, you are everywhere.

Revel in ubiquity you vessel of antiquity

Promise of tomorrow, proof of yesterday

60 million years defying evolution.

Oh possum, confusing muse of sages through the ages

Once you shared the stage with dinosaurs

Were linked with scores of smarter species gone extinct

Were on the brink, yourself, a time or two

And yet, somehow, beneath that brow

Shines bright the light of

NOW

Next, we have a poem telepathically transmitted by the possum poet Apple and entitled "Applesauce."

Applesauce. Applesauce and dirt

I like my foot

Dark, blankie, sleeeeep, OW!

Applesauce, blankie

Sauce

Amanda Gorman, eat your heart out. This brilliant turn was accompanied on the bongos by the poet, herself. No bongos? No worries. An original hand-carved West African djembe from Guinea will do in a pinch. And don't forget to snap, sixties style. Snapping in the presence of poets is a sign of reverence and awe. Regardless of what you may hear, it never goes out of style.

The next poem was contributed by the late great Lloyd Heslip, known in literary circles as Pigfoot. It's titled "I've Seen the Best Minds of My Generation Play Possum."

> Nocturnal creature caught in the light
>
> Practice neither flight not fight
>
> Lay down, play dead, play possum
>
> It's a board game, it's a dance
>
> Teachers standing around students at a prom, saying,
>
> "Billy, Sally, put down your hands and arms and get up."
>
> Billy snores, while Sally exits on all fours.

And now "Oh Opossum," from Scout the Husky:

> Opossum, you are so awesome
>
> Who knows what you think or have done
>
> Contemplating where to eat and where to sleep
>
> The opossum asks not another creature for its keep
>
> Though the opossum be limited in years
>
> He is still good company to converse with
>
> While eating some chips.

From the poet known only as Margaret, "Haiku for a Thursday in Autumn":

This opossum joy

So many hours on YouTube

I have lost my job

By now some of you are thinking, *I wanna play*! *I could write a brilliant possum poem.*

Do it, then. Do it and submit your possum poem, squirrel sonata, rodent rhapsody, marsupial madrigal, sugar glider serenade, rat rondeau, capybara composition, marmoset epithalamium, or hamster haiku to our website, MEpearl.com, and maybe see yourself featured in our next book, *Pearls Before Swine*. No offense.

Bath, Grooming, and Beauty

A CONSTANT CONCERN FOR MANY OF YOU IS, "WHAT DO I DO IF I can't get to a proper possum grooming salon because my car is filled with a passel of nursing joeys who can't be disturbed until they are old enough to be on their own?" We all know how long that can take. In larger metropolitan centers, many of your marsupial supply outlets provide taxi services to and from their spas. But what if your possum looks ragged on a Thursday when public possum services are unilaterally closed in protest over a universal lack of respect?

That's when it's important to know the home emergency ABCs of proper possum bath and beauty procedures and products.

First: make your opossum feel secure by placing a no-slip mat on the bottom of the basin.

Next you'll want to apply petroleum jelly to protect the eyes. But don't. Petroleum is a controversial product (look it up), so forget it. Instead, use a no-tears shampoo.

You always want to test the water carefully because the opossum's body temperature is lower than ours, so what feels warm to you may be too warm for them. Once the proper temperature is established, you'll want to keep a frothing thermometer close by to maintain that temperature throughout the procedure. Now squeeze an ample sample of shampoo into your palm, rub yours hands together vigorously, and lather up your little friend all over, reaching every nook and cranny while being careful to avoid the eyes. Possums are dandy little swimmers[10] and have a natural protection that closes off the inner ear from excess water. Remember that old wives' tale that says, "Never put anything smaller than your elbow into your ear?" It's true. Don't do it.

You can wipe off the outer ear gently with a soft cloth, but deeper cleansing is best left to a veterinarian and never, ever to a Q-tip.

Depending on your possum's lifestyle you may wish to include a gentle tail scrub using a natural loofah or exfoliating sea sponge. Spare no expense on these bath and beauty products. After all, doesn't your opossum deserve the best? Now it's time to rinse off with filtered lukewarm water, then pat dry with a clean, absorbent shammy towel, being sure to get the underbelly and upper chest so that your opossum doesn't catch a chill, because nobody wants that.

I like to finish with a moisturizing conditioner to give that coat a super lustrous shine. My conditioner of choice is honeysuckle rain

10 Don't test this out.

because, honestly, I prefer natural fragrances when it comes to wildlife. And, as I'm sure you'll agree, there is nothing more satisfying than a clean, fresh, sweet-smelling opossum. Am I right? Go ahead, bury your face in the belly of that squeaky-clean baby. You know you want to. Inhale deeply. Dee-lightful!

Many of you are probably using mini brush rollers for after-shampoo styling, and that's just fine. But, and I cannot emphasize this enough, do not put hair extensions on an opossum. No.

It's sometimes difficult maneuvering mini rollers for that carefree spit curl effect, but keep at it. The results are so worth it. I usually recommend against permanent waves, but if you must give your opossum a perm, use the kind without peroxide, which can irritate their sensitive skin, and, as always, never use a product that has been tested on animals. Don't do that.

When the process is complete, hold a magnifying mirror up to the possum and chant:

"Mirror, mirror, in my hand, Who's the prettiest, bestest, most spectacular possum in the land?

You are!" They just love that. Sets their little tails to wagging, as you'll see.

NOTHING ABNORMAL AROUND HERE

Proper Possum Exercise and Fitness

IN TRUTH, NO ONE HAS EVER ASKED ME, "GEORGETTE, HOW DO YOU stay so trim and fit?"

But if they did, I would have a one-word answer: "Possercizing." This is the ultimate fitness routine, meeting all of your exercise needs plus those of the domestic possum. Sound too good to be true? Well, just read along and get caught up in the magic. It's always so wonderfully bonding when you can share activities with your possum and a workout regimen is a prime example. Best that you not try to join them on the exercise wheel. Not only will your movements be inhibited, but they will resent the intrusion.

Elliptical machines are fun but may prove addicting to the possum who cannot keep up with a treadmill. Think outside the cage;

multidimensional cross-fit training with long-term goals, but no longer than three years.[11]

For a fully graduated effect begin with two possums around 187 grams each. Take a baby possum in each hand with elbows bent at a 90 degree angle and begin gently jogging to "Oh Fields, My Fields" from the Alexandrov Ensemble's *Best of the Red Army Choir*. Gradually work up to nine and three quarter pound possie weights while jogging to "Ride Cossack, Ride!" by the Russian Philharmonic. Always keep a first aid kit handy when working with live weights. Also, plenty of quick energy snacks like bananas for potassium and raw liver for any traumatic blood loss.

Beginning to think yoga is more your style? You'll need a yoga mat for you and your favorite possum, unless you prefer to rough it and stretch out on Mother Nature's blanket of dirt, sticks, and organic waste.

If you look good, you feel good, and if you feel good, you do good, so don't stint on those adorable matching yoga outfits, which are featured at your local marsupial supply outlet. Look for the label Pearl of Paris.

Possum/person yoga requires deeply connected psyches. You and your possum remain separate while becoming one, yet two, of the same essence though honoring the boundary between that which makes up the illusion of "other." The enlightened joining of essences who by their nature must remain disconnected isolates. Later I shall explain The Trinity, but for now it is from the uno-duo-uno perspective that we shall enter the asanas.

Roll your possum into a ball and hold her there for fifteen seconds.

---

11 Average life span of the opossum. Working with a dead possum is possible but can be depressing and is not recommended.

Bingo baffle, Bob's your waffle, dead bug pose! Unroll the possum and fold her up into the half-tortoise, stretch out her right leg into the bird of paradise, then lift the tail into the reverse cobra and uncoil slowly into downward facing dog. Now place a generous slab of peanut butter on your possum's tongue to achieve the lion pose, which will loop well beyond the fifteen seconds required to make a pose legit. Finally, you can end the session by flipping up the yoga ensemble and exposing the possum's rump in a salutation to the moon. Given the intricate interconnectedness of you and your possum, both spirits are now considered complete . . . until tomorrow when it all begins again. Namaste.

Possum-Speak

HAAAAH RRRRR TSH TCHE TSSSSSSS.
Just sit with that for a while. Really take it in.

Alien Alert

THIS MAY BE THE MOST IMPORTANT SEGMENT IN THE BOOK, SO PAY attention. I know that you are concerned about being taken over by aliens. Who isn't? But, like everything else, there are good aliens and bad aliens. We've all heard that your dog is the best judge of character and, when it comes to people, that's probably true. But, when it comes to extraterrestrials, only your possum knows for sure.

Opossums have many extraordinary abilities; they can ward off rabies with their low body temperature, survive the most poisonous snakebite, *and* they know a bad-faith alien when they see one.

Prove it to yourself by purchasing some evil alien action figure, like a Gorn or a Xenomorph, online. Wind it up, turn it on, and let it rip near your opossum, who will immediately show signs of discomfort, alerting you that this otherworldly entity is up to no good and that you should get the hell out of Dodge. Wouldn't want a scorpion from outer space tearing through your chest like they did to John Hurt, now would you? There's one poor puppy who sure could have used an opossum.

But what about the tardigrade, the space-loving water bear? Have you reached a conclusion, or are you still undecided about the potential malevolence or benevolence of this Beanie Baby anomaly? A quick marsupial check-in tells you all you need to know.

If you are, Goddess forbid, a household without an opossum, *run*, don't walk, to your nearest shed, dumpster, or marsupial supply outlet and chase one down today. Commandeer that creature and put it in uniform. Nothing like a stinkin' badge to scare the slime out of a bad alien.

If some unspeakable tragedy requires you to rehome your opossum, consider the Roswell UFO Festival as a hotspot of potential adopters. Just flash those canny rock star features and bingo baddie, Bob's your daddy!

Portrait of the Artist as a Young Possum

It is an irrefutable fact that within each possum burns the angst of the artist yearning to be free. And so it is incumbent upon you to provide them with all the art supplies you can lay your hands on. Like brushes, although the true artist will prefer to use her own tail. You should have a wide variety of food colorings available, including the more subtle pastels, and, of course, canvases—many, many, many canvases. Later, when we explore "the dance" and site-specific expressions, your opossum will be using her body as the brush and the surrounding environment as the canvas.

When Pearl and I eventually get into "opossum as thespian" in a future book or video, we'll be focusing on Restoration and Elizabethan theater along with Commedia dell'arte. Obviously, you'll need an assortment of costumes.

If you are short on art supplies, rectify that immediately. Bookmark this page and hightail it to the art department of your local marsupial supply outlet. Call ahead: these items move quickly.

If there were an elephant in the room, it would be the Phoenix Zoo's Ruby, with her pallet and brush. Now *there* was a self-actualized elephant, despite all those years in prison on a chain gang. And how about those Wegman Weimaraners, eh? What extraordinary installation artists!

Opossum art goes back before recorded time. Of course, there's no record of that. Let's take a look at this exquisite canvas painted by Peach Opossum back in the day.[12]

---

12 Pet peeve of Georgette. Back in *what* day? This is the day. Today. Today will always be my day. And yours.

PUDDING AND ME

Here the artist mixes the more vibrant earth tones with tapioca. Hence the title, *Pudding and Me*. Notice the endearing and unrestrained vitality, the delicate interplay of light and shadow, the humorous blending of taupe and mauve. Peach offers a storied vision of her world in which environmental forces and human culture might be harnessed and subdued in a joyful affirmation of zoological rapprochement.[13]

Other opossums currently residing in the ME Pearl Marsupiary are less temperamental and dead, and will happily accept commissions for abstracts or landscapes that match your furniture and complement your wall.

And now for "the dance," which will require a warm-up, naturally. *Four-five-six-seven-jette, jette, jette, relevé pirouette, entre cote, tombée, élevée, entre chat, entre chat, entre chat, et oiseau est morte, relevé deux trois quatre, arabesque et bingo boncle, Robert est ton oncle!*

Mostly we consider "the dance" gender fluid, but if you would like to pattern your opossum's terpsichorean training on extant icons, here's a leaping off point: the interpretive dance *à la* Isadora Duncan. The first time through, the opossum will need your assistance. See bracketed instructions.

I am Ashera, tree of life [stand on hind legs commanding space]

In a breeze [sway] in a blizzard [shake] in a hurricane [wild improvisation]

I am a bird [fly or perch]

The bluebird of happiness [clip on blue feather]

I am Astarte, Goddess of the Heavens [lift way up]

I am the Wheel of Time [cartwheel and spin]

---

13 This painting sells for $3,900 plus S&H, or make an offer.

I am Gaia, Mother Earth. See, I give birth and I nourish and flourish and thrive [clip on blossom]

Then I wither and perish, no longer alive [drape with black scarf]

It's the loss of the leaf, of the feather and blossom [sniff]

But don't cry for me, Jules Feiffer [whip off black scarf]

I was just playing possum. [Deep curtsy]

Always applaud your opossum's creative efforts. It inspires them to even greater heights.

And now for an homage to Vaslav Nijinsky: That most opossums share Nijinsky's intense personal charisma is a given, but you may be surprised to learn how many can replicate his gravity-defying leaps. Really. It's uncanny.

Go ahead, fill the room with Claude Debussy's "Prélude à l'aprèsmidi d'un faune" and hurl your opossum high into the air and watch how long it hovers there, weightless.

Our revels now are ended.[14] These our actors,

As I foretold you, were all spirits and

Are melted into air, into thin air[15]

---

14 William Shakespeare, *The Tempest*, act 4, scene 1.

15 Takeaway: So resist getting too attached. Everything vanishes and was probably not real to begin with.

Emergency Preparedness

WELL, HERE WE ARE IN THE TWENTY-first CENTURY AND WE'VE all heard dire predictions, from the end of the Mayan calendar, Nostradamus's descriptions of doom, solar implosions, polar shifts, takeover by aliens, the Illuminati, pandemic viruses, collision with the planet Nibiru, to say nothing of the appearance of the Antichrist. *Il faut faire attention*, eh?

We know you don't like to think about it, but it's important to put together an emergency plan and a whole boatload of medical supplies in case that plan fails. We're here to help.

You'll need a waterproof disaster kit into which you'll put a nonperishable tin of sardines, jar of caviar, bag of dry cat food, cans of fruits and vegetables, pecan-flavored energy drink (helps the medicine go down), along with, of course, water, at a pint per possum per day.

I recommend springing for a professionally packed first aid case, which you can find at any marsupial supply outlet. Don't forget to include the number of your veterinarian along with extra doses of your possum's prescription medications and duplicate copies of their birth certificates, health records, and proof of medical, dental, vision, and natural disaster and calamitous event insurance.

And of course, always have a recent 8 x 10-inch photo of your possum available for posting in case you and your possum become separated.

The photo should accurately reflect the appearance of the opossum. Last year's glamor shot will be useless in an emergency.

Keep the exercise wheel oiled up. It will be a good enrichment activity while you're waiting for the rescue team to dig you out.

Should your possum go into cardiopulmonary arrest, you'd best know possum CPR and have "Stayin' Alive" by the Bee Gees cued up in iTunes.

Quick brush up: interlock your fingers and press down on the sternum for fifteen compressions followed by the breath of life, mouth-to-mouth resuscitation, where you pinch off the opossum's nostrils and exhale directly into her or his open mouth two times.[16] Keep this up until the animal revives or you expire, whichever comes first.

During an emergency it's important to bolster your possum's courage and confidence any way you can. Remember the "Opossum Marching Song"? That's a trick question. There isn't an "Opossum

---

16 This technique is specific to the Virginia opossum and should not be used on other marsupials.

Marching Song," because opossums know that the best tactic in a true emergency is to just lay down and play dead. But what if *you* want to be more proactive? Why not take CERT (Community Emergency Response Team) training? Join the rescue team and lead the search for less fortunate opossums who may not have a proper opossum emergency preparedness plan in place.

Disaster psychology can be an intricate and sensitive issue for the opossum, and we'll be covering that another time for those who survive. Meanwhile, remember that the opossum who prepares this way may live to play dead another day.

Tying the Knot

WE'RE GOING TO TAKE YOU THROUGH THE PREPARATION AND execution of an elegant upper-class opossum wedding, with all the trimmings. When it comes time for your opossums to plight their troth, you'll know how it's done properly.

The union of Potato—Pomme de Terre in foreign markets—and Passion Fruit was the wedding of the century, outshining that of Meghan and Harry, Charles and Diana, even Luke and Laura. This was the real deal. At least, that was the intention. Being Anglophiles, we wanted all the pomp and circumstance that a well-brought-up opossum would know to expect. But everyone's eagerness to get to the cakes, his, hers, and mine, eclipsed most of that. No matter—I was just so grateful that this young couple elected not to live in sin as most wildlife regrettably do.

Potato sported a top hat and tails along with a white tie and silver waistcoat. Passion Fruit was wrapped in miles of eggshell tulle in an attempt to replicate Diana's train. It worked magnificently. As mother of everyone and official officiant, I wore floor-length peach chiffon with a corsage of wisteria. I considered lilies, but that flower is poison to many animals and since the wedding party would soon be drunk off their buns, it wasn't worth the risk.

Both bride and groom wrote their own vows and, while less eloquent than hoped for, we were happy to be regaled with their heartfelt rhetoric. Potato began with a guttural grunt and the unmistakable sentiment, "Me want female." Crude, but not without a certain primitive charm. Passion Fruit followed with high-pitched squeals and the unmistakable sentiment, "*Help! Help!* Somebody get me outta here." Not what you expect a young bride to say on her wedding day, at least not out loud. Actually, there were several unsettling aspects to these nuptials, including evidence that rodents had gotten to the cakes. But we ate the one less nibbled on, and that made all the difference. Don't you just hate those weddings where they make you wait for the cake? Don't wedding planners know that everyone's head is going, *yada, yada, yada, blah, blah, blah, where's the cake*? Well, this wedding had a major cake break right in the middle. Take a lesson.

And then it was my turn to shine. "And so," I said, "with the power vested in me, Georgette Spelvin, by Pearl and the Universal Life Church . . . ." (Really, it's very cool. You just send them money and they send back official documents certifying that you are a reverend. And if it's written down, it must be true. I can even make people saints, and have. Personally, I would have passed over Junípero Serra, but that's all blood under the bridge now.)

"Does Mr. Elephant have the ring?" He did not. I won't say that Mr. Elephant spoiled the wedding, but he did. He began trumpeting in low frequency with the unmistakable sentiments, "Unnatural! Inappropriate! Anthropomorphizing!" What a Mr. Party Poop.

But I press on, "If anyone here besides the bride and the elephant know of any reason—"

"Arooooooouhhh.   PHNEEEEEE   PAWOO," continues Mr. Elephant.

"Yada, yada, yada. Blah, blah, blah," continue I. "I now pronounce you Jill and Jack and may you have a passel of little joeys."

"*Arooooooouhhh. PHNEEEEEE PAWOO!*" Translation: "No indiscriminate breeding! Of anything! Especially guests!" Weddings have reputations. Takeaway: Don't get married with an elephant in the room.

Conscious Uncoupling

ALL THAT POMP AND CIRCUMSTANCE DIDN'T WORK OUT AS WELL as we'd hoped. Luckily they got a package deal where every wedding comes with a free divorce. Let this be a life lesson, especially to those of you marrying in May.

So now we turn our attention to the conscious uncoupling of Potato—that's Pomme de Terre—and his briefly blushing bride,

Passion Fruit. Did you see this coming? 'Cause really, I didn't. I paid a lot for that mother of everybody dress and then had to turn it into lots of little hammocks.

But it's okay, because what undoing of a problematic proper possum pagan pawfasting would be complete without a conscious uncoupling cake? Not ours! Our cake was decorated with animal species the newly freed couple could consider dating as they take their separate paths into the happily ever after.

We had a rat (significantly smarter than the opossum . . . and you, for that matter, thoughthat wouldn't be a problem because neither you nor the opossum would ever be likely to recognize that) and a serpent—a surprisingly appropriate partner because possums are immune to most snake venoms. A little kerfuffle won't kill the honeymoon or the beloved. And we had the ever popular bat. A word of warning, here. Bats, unlike possums, *are* rabies vectors, but their teeth are so tiny you may not notice you've been bitten. So be sure and take extra care when grooming your bat.

You'll be relieved to know that this union was never consummated, and even if it had been it would not have resulted in baby joeys since Potato did take the responsible precautions.

I asked the divorce guests to join me in celebrating the couple's choice to remain civil and respectful as they took the high road, putting aside all differences and honoring the contribution of the other. And if possums are known for anything, it's for their generosity of spirit.

First, Passion was asked to share her high-minded parting sentiments. Instead she delivered a low blow, but it's worth recording for posterity.

"Back off, you jacked up sack o' Jell-O! I am a powerful passionate possum and I don't need a potato to make me whole."

"Well said, Ms. Fruit," said I. That bears repeating.

Will all of you ladies reading this now repeat aloud, "I don't need a potato to make me whole"? Louder.

I don't need a potato to make me whole.

I can't hear you.

I DON'T NEED A POTATO TO MAKE ME WHOLE.

When you read this at book club, I recommend you all joining hands at this part and raising a chant till you drop to the floor in exhaustion.

Potato's reply was not unexpected. These things smart.

"Well, aren't you just the prissy little possie princess! Such a baby! It would take a joeyophile to put up with you. You think you're so special, but there are plenty more possums in the tree, Lil' Missy."

He later had this embossed onto place mats, which he gave her as a going away gift. Then, with the power vested in me by the Omnipresent Pearl, I severed the tie that bound the two together for less than a day. It was more of a leash and double harness made specifically for this purpose and available by special order through your local marsupial supply outlet. Check the return policy prior to purchase.

It was then time to divvy up the assets beginning with Mr. Elephant, the all-pervasive voice of reason, and who wouldn't want that?

Potato didn't. Passion Fruit didn't. And I didn't. Let's face it, nobody wants to be responsible for the elephant in the room.

Opossum as Service Animal: Pros and Cons

About 26 percent of all Americans have a disability, and there's an increasing demand for service animals to assist with day-to-day activities. If you have a disability, excellent organizations exist for the purpose of matching you with the animal best suited to meet your needs, and frequently at no cost to you. Now, I know what you're thinking: "I want a dog!" Well, of course you do. But I want you to reconsider because the better choice may be—that's right—the service opossum, and here's why: there are no long waiting lists for a service opossum, no inconvenient mandatory training sessions, and they're fairly easy to find. Just roam through your neighborhood alleys after dark and scavenge through trash cans. No need to feel funny. Lots of people do this.

Once your mission is accomplished, take her or his measurements and purchase a spiffy service vest at your local marsupial supply outlet. Many states do not require certification for service animals and this is good news, because testing will only stress your possum unduly.

I think we are most familiar with animals who assist the visually impaired by guiding their partner through the complexities of pedestrian traffic and public transportation. Here I must warn you against setting your expectations too high.

Another service performed by animals is incipient seizure detection and warning. For example, if I were about to have a seizure, the opossum might sense this and tap my hand to remind me to take my medication, which many readers may suspect I've not been doing. Opossums can get your attention in many ways; nudging, peeing on your arm, or just nipping you can all be effective.

If you have a disability, you have enough to think about without adding rabies, so here's the good news: no matter how hard or how often that opossum may bite you, you will not contract rabies, because their body temperature is too low to harbor the virus. Isn't that good news? Of course, it is.

For the hearing-impaired, opossums can be trained to turn their heads in the direction of a noise. Fire alarms may not register for an opossum, but someone yelling "*SHARK!*" surely will, so you and your opossum can swim in the ocean with confidence. Anything more startling and the opossum may just roll over and play dead, not the most helpful behavior in an emergency.

Another category of importance is the psychiatric service animal for those with mental and emotional disabilities. Opossums make excellent confidants. If you see a service animal with a disabled person, do not approach that animal. This is not a pet. It is a working member of a team doing an important job. Any attempt to distract that animal could prove harmful to her partner, so don't do it. No. Just no. That's a hard no.

Now, in closing, there are some disadvantages to a service possum. They're short-lived, so by the time you are both fully trained and bonded you have maybe a good month before they drop dead. For real. This can be distressing, especially to those with an emotional disability. Also, opossums can turn on a dime and become aggressive, but only if they get upset, and that would be your fault, wouldn't it? So be really careful not to upset them and this won't happen, probably.

Always give your opossum the benefit of the doubt. Just remember, no possum is perfect and neither are you. Next time you or someone you know is in the market for a service animal, think outside the box. Your answer may be right in your own backyard, or somewhere down the alley, or in the supermarket dumpster where she or he may be mistaken for food. Maybe start there so you can consider the animal as a rescue. Rescue animals make the best . . . everything.

Disposal Techniques

Now it's time to talk about proper opossum disposal. How often have you found yourself with a dead opossum, wondering, *What do I do now?* I know. Be not dismayed. You have options. Many cities have dead animal pickup, but this can seem impersonal. You may be inclined to simply dig a hole and put the animal in it, but, oddly enough, that can be illegal. Ironic that you can be despicably cruel to a possum and suffer no consequences other than the ruination of your soul, but to bury that animal you would risk significant fines and potential jail time.

When Peach Possum, long-time star of the ME Pearl Productions Proper Opossum Care video series, passed away of natural causes (if dying of old age at three can be considered natural), we faced the proper opossum disposal dilemma. Peach was adorable! She was so reminiscent of one of those darling Disney characters that it wasn't surprising we followed the lead of Walt himself and considered cryogenics (that's freezing her head).[17] But it seemed so cold.

Instead, we decided to employ the services of a very classy, very pricey pet mortuary located in Southern California (no surprise there). This facility offered multiple amenities along with cremation.[18] This was the go-to for dead pets when you care enough to spend a substantial sum to get the very best; like a lump of clay with a paw print, a Ziploc baggie of ashes, and a generic condolence card. Yes, a choice you can feel good about.

I am not suggesting that you call in a boutique mortuary for just any opossum you see lying dead by the side of the road. No, that would be excessive. But, speaking of opossums lying dead by the side of the road, if you see one, you're going to want to stop and check the pouch for living babies. *Yes,* you *are*! Reach inside, don't be afraid to go deep, and gently feel around for moist little squirmy things. Obviously, this must be done barehanded. If you are lucky enough to feel stirrings of life, get the towel you keep in your car for just such occasions. Failing this, you can use the shirt off your back and carefully wrap the dead mother with the living babies still attached and deliver this sacred bundle to your local animal shelter or, better yet, to a professional wildlife rehabilitator. And here is some more good news: chances are that all of those babies can be saved.

---

17 The existence of Walt's frozen head is in dispute.

18 Today we recommend aquamation for both sentimental and environmental reasons. Check to see if it is legal in your state. If not, consider becoming an activist. Aquamation is an excellent alternative for people as well, although our ultimate preference is a conservation burial. For more information visit the website of an organization called The Order of the Good Death.

When it comes time for our current "and company" to make their transitions, I'm considering the ever-popular companion animal taxidermy, made famous by Roy Rogers and his horse, Trigger. That was the horse that got stuffed, not Roy. Although, I'm not really sure about Roy.

> So, a veterinarian and a taxidermist go into business together. Their slogan: "Either way, you get your dog back."

If you decide on taxidermy, you'll want to select a pose that best depicts the soul-truth of your possum passé and be sure to arrange it just so before rigor mortis sets in.

Does your spirit yearn for a ritualistic send-off? Try this on for size. Collect a colander of rose petals, one white candle, a pack of matches, a goblet of holy water,[19] a hamster wheel, a pot of fresh dirt, your possum's favorite incense, a Sakura folding fan with tassel, Psalm 22, and a Pakistani flautist. Think of the dead possum as an opportunity to bridge the worlds. I like to think that whenever a possum passes away an angel gets her wings.

Remember, the following ceremony is powerful and must not be entered into whimsically. It's a good idea to rehearse the ritual on a predeceased opossum so that you don't inadvertently dispatch your beloved companion to the Depths of Sheol.

---

19 If you say it's holy, it's holy.

Hopefully your predeceased ringer possum will get the idea and do what comes naturally: play dead.

Lay the animal out on a bed of dirt and sprinkle with rose petals. Ad lib by Pakistani flautist. You'll want to read some parting sentiments, hence Psalm 22. However, since most possums are presumably Druid, you may prefer a passage from *The Pagan Book of Living and Dying*.

(Waft incense and flutter fan) May the air carry your spirit gently.

(Strike match and light candle) May the flame release your soul

(Dip fingers in holy water and flick hither and thither) May the water cleanse you of all pain and suffering

(Throw dirt on dead body) May the earth receive you

(Spin hamster wheel) May the wheel turn and turn again and bring you home

Know that you are loved and can never be replaced
(Replace predeceased opossum with dead one and begin again)
You may want to bookmark this page for easy reference.

And don't be too quick to dismiss the dramatically satisfying Viking funeral. Google for instructions.

Think we've exhausted the options? Think again. We saved the last for last. Cloning. Do you just love your possie-wossie so much that you can't imagine life without her/him? Then maybe cloning is for you. But there are other further reaching reasons to take Somatic Cell Nuclear Transfer seriously.

I am sure that everyone reading this shares the concern, the dread even, that with climate change, deforestation, environmental pollution, and rapidly disappearing habitats, the magnificent possum may soon go extinct. Are they on the endangered species list? Well, no. Do we trust the people in charge of making these lists and protecting endangered species? We know only that we can trust Pearl. After that, we must trust the science.

Remember Dolly the sheep? Well, Dolly didn't have to do Dallas to make little dollies. Not this time. Nature was preempted by science, and baby Dolly was conceived in a petri dish. I think. Doesn't matter. Dolly was already six years old when she was born. Think about it. I'm not completely sure how this works, but we've heard of a discrete little biotech company online—you can probably do the same thing cheaper through Amazon—where they send you a swab that you use to collect DNA-rich saliva from whatever/whomever you want and return it in the envelope provided, along with "price subject to change." Cheap at the price when you think of it. And bingo buncle, Bob's your uncle, they send you back a *clone* of anything, including yourself. So, if you are having trouble finding love . . . just sayin'. When the happy day arrives and your matching possum is delivered, be sure and check it over thoroughly. You don't want a pouch where a pecker oughta be. That's not cloning, that's fraud. This is an industry rife with corruption and I'm sorry I brought it up.

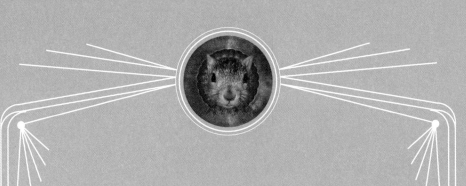

PART THREE

And Now for a Change of Pace

How to Age Beef

A LITTLE BACKGROUND: THIS WAS ORIGINALLY INTENDED AS A video. I was doing research on proper opossum nutrition online and discovered that most information concerned cooking the possum, not cooking *for* the possum. In my meanderings I found a plethora of tutorials on how to age beef and realized what a popular topic that must be. And I thought, *I know how to do that. Nothin' to it.*

But I needed a freestanding cow, which is more difficult to find than you might imagine. I thought I could just drive along a rural road, play a few licks on my recorder, and the cows would come running. Alas, cow farmers are a suspicious lot. Sign after sign read, "Trespassers Will Be Shot." Guess they were worried someone might tip the cows. And I would have tipped the cows, generously, for services rendered, but it wasn't worth getting shot.

I have friends who run farm animal sanctuaries, and there is no shortage of refugee cows, but just try getting access during a pandemic. No amount of begging or bribing would budge a keeper of the cows. So, I decided to scrap the video and put the material into this book.

Slowly approach the bovine in question and begin haranguing.

"Oh Lewis, Lewis, Lewis—whatever will I do with you? You'd give me gray hair if I weren't genetically immune. Stress, my cow, stress is what puts us in an early grave. You're killin' me, here, Lewis."

Every day I come to give you these pep talks and every day you just look more downtrodden, dilapidated, and forlorn. You never won a ribbon, you never won a race, you ain't never caught a rabbit. You ain't no friend of mine.

Legally you are property, Lewis. I could sell you to the circus. But they wouldn't want you. You're a one-trick cow. With no trick.

All the other cows face north. That's how cowherders find their way home. Or locate their favorite constellations. But not Lewis. *No.* Sometimes he faces east, sometimes west, sometimes southwest. He just spins to his own drummer.

Everybody said, "Eat Lewis, eat Lewis. It's all he's good for." I was appalled. Eat my buddy Lewis? How could I?

"He'll come around," I said. "Just wait," I said.

You never came around, Lewis, and you never will come around. You are a lost cause and I regret the day I birthed you, and so would your mom if she were around to see what never became of you. And your poor dad. Did you ever wonder why he didn't trot you around the stockyards bellowing "That's my boy!"? Because he was ashamed, Lewis.

Your parents didn't die of mad cow disease. I said that to spare you. They died of *shame*, Lewis.

Well, I've reached the end of my tether. No more Ms. Nice Guy. You fart and you burp and you fill the whole world with methane. You, Lewis, are what's killing the planet. You.

I'm going to leave you now to think about what I've said. Really, let it sink through that worthless hide into those dry and brittle bones. Loser!

Walk away from bovine shaking your head in disgust. Don't look back.

And that, my friends, is how you age beef.

A Word to Hunters

KARMA, BUDDY, KARMA.

Faux Fur Follies

I HAVE A BEAUTIFUL FAUX SEAL FUR COAT THAT IS SPECTACULAR. I love wearing the coat. Summer, winter, fall, spring, doesn't matter. I just love the coat.

But it is very upsetting how many people come up and ask if it's real fur. How could anyone who knows me think that I would wear a coat that rightfully belongs to its original owner? I mean, who but Satan's minions wears real fur anymore? Think about it.

Recently, at a party, I was wearing the coat when a young man of my acquaintance came up and, yup, asked if it was real fur. Well, it was one time too many, you know? I snapped. I simply snapped, in my fashion, and I said, with the biggest smile ever, "Why yes, Jeffery," that was his name, Jeffery, "Yes, Jeffery, it is. I bashed the baby seals myself.

"Shhh, keep this on the downlow, but . . . there's a Canadian cruise line that offers discreet excursions where guests get to bash their own seals. Otherwise, it's a typical cruise offering the traditional amenities with this one extra . . . perk.

"Don't go, Jeffery. I've just gotten started. You're awakened at the crack of dawn, and after a lovely continental breakfast you are provided with an insulated jumpsuit and a club. You are then taken to one of the more active ice floes where you can leisurely meander about until you spot a mother nursing a pup with a particularly appealing pelt. Once you've made your decision you just march right up and club the hell out of that little sucker. It can be quite a workout, believe you me. Mom won't do much. She just gets out of the way and cries. Oh, buck up, Jeffery. Beauty requires sacrifice. When the deed is done, and there's no hurry, you raise your club and a runner comes and tags your trophy, easy peasy, and then escorts you back to the boat where you'll find a fresh change of clothes, which you'll need, and a hot toddy. Brrrr. It can sure get cold on those ice floes. I must go on because you asked, Jeffery, and I want to give you a full explanation.

"Later, crew members go out and collect the tagged carcasses, which are then expertly prepared by the ship's peltier and presented to participating guests at the captain's dinner. Some guests prefer to cure the pelts with their own urine, and there's ample opportunity for that. Sound good? Hmm? Well, it's not for everyone. Sit down, Jeffery. There's more.

"First timers, and you would be one of those, usually go in a group with a guide and do what is whimsically called a "gang up and bang up" where everyone gets in a good bash or two. In that case you don't come away with a coat, of course. Maybe earmuffs or a key chain. And trust me, you won't lose your keys when they're attached to a lucky seal flipper. Not bloody likely.

"What's the matter, Jeffery? You look a little peaked. Come sit by me. We'll speak of other things. No, really. I insist! There, now. How are the kids? Oh, I'd love to see pictures. Aren't they *adorable*! How old are they now? Five-year-old twin girls. That's just perfect. Perfect. Because this is a "family friendly" event. Yes it is. Children under seven, like your sweet little girls, are provided with *batakas*—foam bats—so they can join in the fun without hurting themselves. They can bash away to their heart's content, creating memories that will follow them for the rest of their lives. It's called "Bop and Stop," and is a perennial favorite. Some families even consider this a rite of passage, rather like a bat mitzvah.

"Can I give you a brochure? Well, suit yourself. But it sure is a fun adventure and who doesn't love a real seal-fur coat? Yes, I think you should go now, Jeffery. You don't look at all well. Thanks for stopping by. Give my love to the kids. Ta."

Idiot! Wait . . . hmm . . . maybe I'm the idiot . . . maybe this is my fault . . . um . . . uh . . . I shouldn't wear this coat at all. Real fur, faux fur, it's still just asking for it. Oh, my beautiful coat. I love you so much. Tomorrow I am giving you to the Wildlife Center to be bedding for newborns. Yes. It's the right thing to do. Because if we stay together, we'll regret it. Oh, maybe not today, maybe not tomorrow, but soon, and for the rest of our lives. We'll always have Canada.

Proper Opossum Perseveration, or Lists and Lists and Lists and Lists and Lists

It's not really about opossums; it's more about names and activities pertaining to opossums. Let me be transparent in writing this chapter. I want you, gentle reader, to take up the torch of the obsessive compulsive and join me in searching out and accumulating absolutely everything that fits into a given category. Dance with me down the path of glazomania.[20]

Beginning with names. In my early days as a wildlife rehabilitator I focused almost exclusively on squirrels. That's what Pearl said to do, so I did. I exhausted names rhyming with Pearl, like Shirley, Early, Earl, Earline, Burl, Hurlbut, Merle, Girly-Girl, Curly, and Surly.

I went into cakes. Seems like an endless category but a good perseverator hangs in until all the options are exhausted. Here is a sampling of the sweetmeats who went through my care. Lady Baltimore, my first

---

20 An unusual fascination with making lists.

pinky. What a miracle watching a little wad of protoplasm grow into a squirrel, or into anything. Then there were Pound and Loaf and Bundt, triplets, Cup and Sheet, Red Velvet, Lemon Chiffon and Angel Food, Pineapple Upside-Down, Fruitcake, Tiramisu, Esterházy, Birthday, Strawberry Short, Carrot and Zucchini, Teacake, Pan and Torte, Battenberg, Rum Cake, Buttercream, Charlotte Russe, honorable mention to Boston Cream and so many more.

Then possums appeared and I became interested in fruit, specifically fruit beginning with the letter *P*. There was Plum, who stayed with us at the Luxor in Las Vegas and got his Egyptian on.

Peach was the majordomo possum when the video program began. Then there was Pear, the Prunes, Pineapple Bob, Persimmon, Pomegranate, Pumpkin, The Apples: Fuji and Crab, Potato (that's Pomme de Terre in foreign markets), Passion Fruit, Papaya, Pomelo, Pamplemousse, and Pawpaw. Also Fig.

Then creatures were coming in with conditions that made them unreleasable, and I opened up the naming process to video viewers who took up the challenge with unexpected fervor and, it turns out, a passionate possessiveness.

We seem to attract tripods at the ME Pearl Marsupiary, sometimes referred to as Gaia's Halfway House, beginning with the divine Pearl, herself. The name submissions sometimes reflected the conditions. Plus, special preference was shown to names beginning with P. You can guess why. There was Peggy, for Peggy Leggy, Eileen (I lean), Tripod, Tripoli, Triple sec, Trident, Trifecta, Triangle, Trapezoid, Paw Paw Paw (three paws), and someone suggested Poker (because she only needed one good hand).

Other submissions included Petite Pois, Persephone, Pamela, Penelope, Peony, Perrier, Pandora, Paloma, Pywacket, Poplar, Pythia (good, but Pearl's the only pithy one around here), Pierrot, Plucky, Prunsie, Primrose, Peppermint, Palimony, Pumpernickel, Periwinkle, Panama, Pita Pocket, Port-a-Potty, PayPal, Peapod, Pepsi, Prickly Pear, Pola Negri, Plops, Poppet, Parsley. Paisley, Pass-port, Cybill Sheridan, Piccadilly, Piccalilli, Pterodactyl, Parfait, Party, Patience, Passion, Promise, Prana, Plefty, Pot Luck, Pastiche, Panache, Panacea, Popsicle, Padonkadonka, Putain (oh, that wasn't nice), Posselina, Papilloma, Janet, Posey, Rosey, Applesauce, Promenade, Pilgrim, Pluto, Pippin, Pontiac, Plymouth, Pythagoras, Pisces, Phoebe, Phaedra, Peggy Sue, Pyramid, Phalange, Popcorn, Lady Fingers, Pepper, Pogo, Palm Palm, Betty, Pina (presumably after Pina Bausch with all those arms), Piña Colada, Peace, Payola, Pylon, Patience, Perseverance, Prudence, Pom Pom, Parade, Delphi, Achilles (problematic foot?), Plantain, Banana, Pleasant, Prospero, Puppy, Plata de Pasta, Playa, Puck, Plucky, Picnic, Proverb, Polaris, Pomodoro, Prom Queen, Poem, Passepartout, Pico, Pariah, Pad-Mae, Patty, Patsy Klein, Plan 9 (from outer space), Playbill, Panama, Pru, Sweet Pea, Trog, Princess, Palmyra, Provolone, Polar, Pleaides, Parsnip, and for a duo Pick-up and Drop-off, Prequel and Sequel, Pacman, Opie, Poppy, Pirate, Pebbles, Bam Bam, Pamela, Presley, Paradise, Terpsichore, Tribble (remember the Trouble with Tribbles?), Pill, Pilates, Palimpsest (something altered but still bearing visible traces of its earlier form, referring to the phantom limb), Problem, 'cause she *has* one, Pickle, 'cause she's *in* one, Prop, 'cause she *is* one, Poet, Pundit, Pistachio, Panini, Spumoni, Greg, Oracle, Orion, Ophelia, Opal, Perseverance, Vera, Dot, Polka, Polka Dot, Polonaise, Pedal Pusher, Pogo Stick, Pringle, Felicity, Peter, Piper, Peck, Pickle, Pepper, Polly, Polydactyl (because who doesn't love irony), Pylon, Prosper, Prius, Pretzel, Primo, Presto, Pesto, Posh, Pasta, Platypus, Pariah, Preface and Postscript, Pandemonium, Pantheon, Predicament, Paranormal, Pantomime, Pentimento, Pastoral, Petrovich, Prototype, Pro Bono, Pentacle, Moxie and Chutzpah, and for a threesome Possible, Probable, and Plausible, Passable and Presentable, Pavlova, Pratt Fall, Prudence, and Priscilla, Queen of the Desert Platter.

Oh, and a special shout-out to Paré, named for the French barber surgeon Ambroise Paré responsible for the advancement of surgical amputation and the design of the prosthesis. A bit too sophisticated for the circumstances but *so good*. The possum in question wound up being named Maple because the name made her ears prick up and she was Canadian. She was also a fractious little twit.

Similar dilemma with a young pair of opossums, one of whom had a single operative eye. For some reason we got into names with the prefix Poly-, like Polyglot, Pollyanna, Polyester Polysorbate, Polypeptide, Pollywog, Pollywally Doodle All Day.

But the best Poly of all: Polyphemus. I assume that most of you have read the *Odyssey*, probably in the original Greek, and you'll remember that Odysseus and his merry band of men made a stopover at one of the Cyclopean Isles ruled by a one-eyed giant named Polyphemus. Polyphemus and Polyester would have been cute together, but instead I went with Parody and Satire, so that the next time someone comments, "Crazy old witch must be off her meds," I can reply, "Parody and Satire, hello!"

Another challenge given viewers was to come up with artistic projects we could spin off of by changing the animal in the title to "opossum." We'll begin with good ones that were just wrong. See if you can tell why.

Play Possum for Me. Really good but really wrong. *A Streetcar named Opossum.* Can't you just see the little floozy? But no. Wrong.

So here we go—*The Girl with the Possum Tattoo, Silence of the Possums, Old Possum's Book of Practical Possums, Possum on a Hot Tin Roof, Puff the Magic Possum, All Possums Go to Heaven, A Possum with No Name, Island of the Blue Possums, Lord of the Possums, Where the Possums Sing, The Maltese Possum, The Story of Possum Billy, The Possum of the Baskervilles, They Shoot Possums, Don't They?, Reservoir Possums, Beauty and the Possum, Possums of August, The Possum of Wall Street, Mighty Possums, Possum Dundee, Crouching Possum, Hidden Possum, A Werepossum in London, High Stakes Possum Racing, One Trick Possum, Day of the Possums, I Know Why the Caged Possum Sings,* and our personal favorite, *Die Flederpossum*. What can you think of that we left out? Send to website: www.MEpearl.com.

And here's a list of descriptive adjectives viewers felt compelled to share. Many suggested that I was a "whack job" for featuring animals who are, and I quote, "disturbing, freaky, ridiculous, deranged, weird, dumb, batshit crazy," oh no wait, that was for me. Here, this is for the possums: "Diseased, dirty, evil, stinking, disgusting, gross, killers, hateful, hideous, odious, useless, ugly, lazy, vicious, vermin, contaminated, threatening, revolting, harmful, infected, mean, offensive, scary, nasty, cursed, nemesis, sickening, rabid, despicable, stupid, creepy, and well, just bad." If you were one of the people who cared enough to express an opinion, please know it was given all of the consideration it deserves. Meanwhile, thank you for sharing.

Here's something sort of fun, in retrospect. COPPA, the Children's Online Privacy Protection Act, is a 1998 US law created to protect the privacy of children under thirteen. Good idea. Seems that online creators were collecting children's information for marketing purposes. Bad idea. So, all internet content specifically targeting children was at risk of being removed. Too bad, so sad. Didn't affect us at ME Pearl. Until it did.

We've always been pleased, if not surprised, that children often enjoyed our programs even though none of the content was ever designed for them. Parody and Satire, hello! And here's *irony*. Nonetheless, featuring live animals and colorful sets categorized us as potentially in breach of COPPA, which would signal the end of life as we were creating it. And so began the search for titles that would be off-putting to children. Plus, a clear message to the children themselves.

"If you are watching this and you are thirteen or under, please listen carefully. We don't love you anymore. We don't want you here. You have to go now. Go on! You need to go away. Away. Go! *Shoo*! It's for your own good. Just get out. Do it while I'm not looking. Oh, don't look back. Don't make me throw rocks at you!"

This was very emotional. Very *White Fang*. Soon after came the following titles, designed to be childproof: "The History of Cloth," "Revival of Ancient Yupik Rituals," "The Rise of Unions in Nonindustrialized Societies," "101 Symptoms of Ennui," "Travel Guide to Bakersfield," "The Lost Art of Bookbinding," "10 Steps to Fiscal Responsibility," "Diseases of the Pancreas," "Proactive Estate Planning," "Scalawags of Skid Row," "Dawn of Dadaism," "Squirrels and the Stockholm Syndrome," "Taxonomy of the Peruvian Mole," "Spinning, For Fun and For Profit," "Opossum's Guide to VCR Repair," "Linus Pauling was Right," "Proper Possum Enucleation," "What You Need to Know Before an IRS Audit," "3 Days to Perfect Gaelic," "Flatware Through the Ages," "Mortuary Management," "A Compendium of 14th Century Italian Madrigals," "Dianetics for Dogs," "The Dangers of Yohimbe Ingestion," "Atlas Shrugged and the Inconsistency of Objectivism," "String Theory for Dummies," "Lady Chatterley's Possum," "A Rodent's Take on the Regan Years," "Overcoming Hippopotomonstrosesquippedaliophobia," "*Consumers Digest* 1984–87," "Possum's Guide to Planning Your Puppy's Funeral." Feel free to submit your own ideas to our website.

McDonald's Unhappiest Meal

I'M GOING TO SHARE WITH YOU SOME OF MY LESS THAN STELLAR adventures in the field of wildlife rehab beginning with an encounter where the rescue animal was already quite beyond hope.

I was living in a small suburban town at the time. It was mid-July of a brutally hot summer and I'd been driving past this roadkill possum for several days. Earlier I'd made sure there were no babies in the pouch and discovered there was no pouch at all, which meant it was a male, although, at this point, it didn't make much difference. Well, the sadness of it all finally got to me; no city employee, no environmentalist, no family member was coming for this dead possum who was being hit by cars repeatedly. So I went home and got a towel and a metal dustpan for scraping and then returned to do the right thing. I arrived at the site to find a young boy on a bicycle. Now, ordinarily one whiff of so pungent a death odor would have sent me on my way but the boy asked what I was doing with the towel and pan and I said, in a rather lofty tone, that I had come to claim the poor creature and give him a decent burial.

The boy said he had seen me around the neighborhood picking up dead squirrels and was this what I did, for a living, presumably. But I said no, that I preferred to find them alive and what I actually did was to look after ill, injured, and orphaned small mammal wildlife until they were old enough, well enough, and strong enough to look after themselves.

He looked at me with wide-eyed wonder and admiration and said, and this is an actual quote, "That's really nice." That's just what he said. He said, "That's really nice." And in that moment I realized that I am now a role model for America's youth, an awesome responsibility when you think about it. There was no turning away.

I then had to scrape up this revolting creature with maggots crawling out of what remained of various orifices, entrails spread all over the outsides, skin curling off his tail and a death stench that would curl the bark off trees and will never leave my nostrils.

I wanted to get away so bad but the kid was watching me, believing in me, holding me up to some standard that I had probably created for myself.

So, holding my breath, I staunchly scraped possum parts off the blistering pavement, wrapped them in the towel, and gingerly placed the whole mess on the passenger seat of my van.

Such a bad idea. The smell is a hundred times worse in the sweltering van. And now the nausea set in but I started up and set off as though I had a plan because, in the rearview mirror, I saw the boy still watching—only now he was giving me a thumbs-up.

I tried not breathing, but that doesn't last very long. So, keeping one hand on the steering wheel, I leaned out the window as far as was humanly possible, gasping for fresh air, but there just wasn't any. The stink was all-pervasive.

I wanted so much to just heave the wretched thing out the window, but I had an image to maintain. Somewhere out there was a boy on a bicycle who believed in my follow-through.

I couldn't chance him coming across the abandoned carcass.

No, I needed some kind of receptacle. Like a public trash

barrel—but there just wasn't any. It was like trying to find a corner mailbox today. Where did they all go?

And then the clouds parted and there it was, like a shiny gift from heaven, this big beautiful barrel with, of all things, a happy face painted right on it. Surely it was a sign. Further inspection revealed this godsend was stationed at the entrance of a McDonald's drive-through.

As inconspicuously as possible, I sidled up to a barrel, took the towel and its grizzly contents, and casually dropped it in. Then, just to look normal, I drove on up and ordered a Happy Meal.

But I could tell from the growing grimace and watering eyes of the order taker that he was picking up on the stench still surging from my van and now from their own little smiley face trash can. I thought this could be serious. Would anyone else even be able to enter the drive-through? No, their business would probably fall off that day. And I felt bad. Then I felt scared. Probably time to beat a hasty retreat to the nearest car wash.

I paid for food I couldn't even look at and reflected that this was probably McDonald's last Happy Meal of the day.

So many ignominious excursions into the trenches of wildlife rehab when you care enough to do your very best, however exiguous.

Mentoring and Being Mentored

HERE'S A BRIEF STORY ON HOW I LEARNED WHAT IT MEANS TO BE A truly great mentor. Hopefully this will resonate with some of you who are mentoring others and/or being mentored yourself; in any discipline, it doesn't matter, the message is the same.

This happened many years ago when I was new to rehabilitating wildlife and fortunate to have an excellent mentor who had been in wildlife rehab for decades and was quite an icon in the extended community. One day I made an egregious error that sent me into an emotional tailspin. Nobody died but it was a close call. So I reached out to my mentor, the late great Nonda S., for the purpose of explaining what had happened and why I had decided to pack it in and give it up. Clearly, I wasn't suited to this vocation and it would be best for everyone if I just left it to people better qualified.

She said that of course it was my decision but first she wanted to tell me about something that had happened to her recently. Seems she was looking after several litters of motherless baby possums and laundry day came around. As an aside, baby possums can be very messy little creatures. They grow out of it and become almost fastidious, like cats, but as youngsters they can be pretty bad. So, she gathered up all the dirty bedding and threw it in the washer. And it wasn't until sometime later she realized that one of the groups of joeys, that's what baby marsupials are called, was missing. She had scooped them up in the bedding without noticing and run them through the wash. Well, that was stunning.

So, rather naively, I asked if they were all right. She paused and then said. *NOOO*. They were NOT all right. By no means, by no stretch were they all right. Clean, yes. But, no.

This highly respected woman, acknowledged as a preeminent authority in the field, had run a bunch of babies through a washing machine, every cycle.

If I had a nickel for every time I've comforted myself with the thought, *At least I never did anything as bad as that* [which, of course, is open to debate] *and she was a superstar*. Her revealing this to me gave me the heart to go on, to reaffirm my commitment to the cause and continue getting better and better as one does through practice and experience.

And now when I mentor others, I make a point of sharing my egregious mistakes because I know how important it is to accept that we are all fallible, and mistakes will be made, and we can pick ourselves up, dust ourselves off, and press on, hopefully, by the grace of Pearl, without killing anyone in the process.

For those of you who may be thinking of writing in to tell me of egregious mistakes that you or someone else has made in animal rescue …DON'T DO THAT. ABSOLUTELY NOT.

NO! Sit down, and have a plate of spaghetti instead.

The Elephant in the Room

THE VAST MAJORITY OF WILDLIFE BELONG OUTSIDE.

If you see them there, leave them there. If you come across an ill, injured, or orphaned wild animal, contact a professional wildlife rehabilitator immediately.

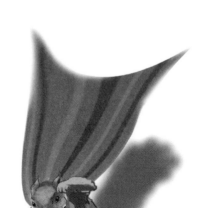

If that's not possible and you are able to transport, take the animal to a shelter or veterinarian, who should have contact information for a rehabber and may even have one on staff. Do whatever you can to create a dark, warm, quiet environment. This means no loud music or see-through containers and PLEASE do not let children or well-meaning adults play with the animal. What's play to humans is literally torture for wildlife and could bring on a condition known as capture myopathy, which is often fatal. So don't foil your own good intentions.

If you do go to a wildlife facility, whether it's multiple buildings or simply a room in someone's home, you are likely to see subtle, or not so subtle, suggestions to make a donation.

People think that since this work requires governmental licensing, it comes with governmental funding. This is not the case. It's all out-of-pocket and it's wildly expensive, often costing several hundred dollars to get a single animal in condition for release. And if veterinary attention is required, the cost is multiplied.

So why do people do it? It's a calling. And the people who can least afford it often hear the loudest call. Go figure. So please, give whatever you can. We are all in this together. However, and I speak for the vast majority of rehabbers, don't let a lack of funds prevent you from bringing an animal to safety. Nobody wants that. We want you to bring the animal in. We want to care for it. The fact that you've taken the time and trouble to get the necessary help is cause to feel really good about yourself.

Now would be a good time to take out your cell phone, find and enter the numbers of your veterinarian, an after-hours emergency veterinarian, your local animal shelter, and the closest wildlife center. Best-case scenario: you'll never have to use them. If you are reading this while driving you get a pass.

PART FOUR

The Spirituality of Squirrel

Psychic Ravings–Uh, Readings, by Pearl

MOST WHO COME FOR PSYCHIC READINGS ARE UNDERAPPRECIATED life-forms, like you, perhaps? I'll let you in on a little secret. This is no big whoop. Anyone can do it. We are all psychic. I can teach you how to read minds and foretell the future in five minutes. But I won't. Because then I wouldn't be so special, would I? I may not be the only dead squirrel on the planet but I'm certainly the most savvy. So, let ME start by bursting your bubble.

Have you ever had a sneaking suspicion that you were Cleopatra or perhaps Napoleon in a former life? Well, the omniscient Pearl is here to tell you that you weren't, so forget it. Let it go. Cleopatra's handmaid? Napoleon's rear guard? No! Not even. But you have been something, unless you are a very new soul, in which case you've been nothing. You know who you are. Probably. And there is nothing wrong with that. But most of the rest of us are really glad we're not you.

Okay, here's a gratuitous message for a male human with the initials L. P. or L. B. You are wondering about changing your lifestyle to one where you will get dirty regularly. You are trying to convince yourself that it would be good for you to simplify and get closer to nature. Sorry L. P. or L. B., it sounds good in theory but in practice it would fall flat. Plus, you'd be taking five others down with you. Stick with what you are good at and clean up your act. It's not your lifestyle that makes you uncomfortable, it's your shoddy work ethic. Fix it. You're welcome.

In the beginning, before I had the code, all my rantings, uh readings, were preceded by a visit to the Akashic Records. I didn't read them so much as sniff and nibble at them. Same result. It's exactly like a visit to Wiki-MyLife only completely different.

Now, with the code, I just beam into your being, find what I want, and beam out before the dogs see me. Sometimes, for appearance's sake, I'm forced to use Georgette as a channel. Might as well play telephone with a kindergarten class. Her whirligig of a filter ejects messages that are barely recognizable as the stable genius raving, uh reading, of ME, Pearl.

You can get pure Pearl all the time when you write into our website and lay your most intimate concerns at my paws, knowing that your privacy is a top-p-p-p prior—OR-OR—AH, I can't say it. So, get the gold by going to MEpearl.com. But, please people, pace yourselves.

Georgette used to take our opossums to another psychic because she couldn't bear the headaches. Ruthie Angel was a hoot. She read paws and did animal card divinations. When Potato opossum kept pulling predators from the pack it became clear he had a suicidal ideation and needed to be kept under close watch. Still, he came home with bags of trinkets and toys and oh, the incense! ME protect us from all that incense.

When asked how Pear, a beloved and mildly deranged family possum, would incarnate next, Ruthie informed everyone that Pear had completed his karma and would ascend into the realm of ME. Oh, pshaw. One doesn't like to contradict Ruthie Angel . . . professional courtesy? Noblesse oblige? Grace of ME? But it's simply not true. He'll be back as a jackal next time. Needs to work it out of his system.

Incoming: Message for Rhonda Fitzhugh from Bridgewater, Connecticut. "Stop it *now*! Everybody knows." And one for Marybelle Sharbett of Flushing, Queens. "In human form you're rather disappointing. But you already know that."

One of the saddest life readings I've done was for an opossum named Apple. A homey. Seems that Apple's incarnation into an opossum was entirely unintended and a big mistake . . . at second sight. Apple was a religious sort and was wanting to return to the earth plane and become a disciple and later an apostle of Jesus Christ. All was going swimmingly during the transition when the unthinkable happened: a hiccup. Instead of projecting apostle into the universe, it came out opossum. And that's what's been looping every three years for the past two thousand years. But I guess she did become an apostle after all, an apostle of ME in the cult of ME, Pearl. Things have a way of working themselves out.

Religion and Politics by Georgette

People are always asking me, "Georgette, what is the political persuasion of the average opossum?" Well, first, is there such a thing as an "average opossum"? I think not. Each possum is an individual with her own mind and set of values.

There are, however, some things on which they all agree. One of the more unfortunate examples is that possums, without exception, disdain wombats, which they regard as an inferior species. Personally, I find this morally reprehensible but they seem stuck on it, for now.

But the underlying question is: Do they lean to the left or to the right? In this current climate of political divisiveness, of course you want to know where the opossum's political loyalties lie. It's probably not what you think. Scratch any possum and you will find an opportunistic anarchist. And that's that. No leaning involved.

"But, Georgette," you may be wondering, "what about the opossum's religious affiliation?" That's really quite simple. Possums are devout followers of the great and powerful Pearl de Wisdom, otherwise known as ME Pearl, the beneficent Pearl, who created the entire multiverse and everything in it, retroactively, because she can do that. It's an unequivocal commitment that you would do well to consider for yourself. If you feel reluctant, purchasing trinkets from our online gift shop is sure to be helpful. There you will find colorful cards that say, "Nothing Abnormal Around Here." Just the thing to send a friend who may need convincing. And, in case you need convincing, the vast majority of possums belong outside. If you see one there, leave it there. If you come across an ill, injured, or orphaned possum, contact a wildlife rehabilitator immediately. If after all this you are still left with a possum, remember communication is key. Rule of thumb: You can never go wrong talking politics or religion.

The Wheel of the Year by Pearl and Georgette

HERE IS THE SECTION THAT WILL CHANGE YOUR LIFE, THAT WILL open up your mind and heart and lung and money clip. Hold that thought. We have arrived at the Wheel of the Year. Enter at any point. This is not your mama's Wheel of the Year. This is RAD, baby.

What better way to ring in the holidays than to provide you with new and better, heretofore unheard-of, holidays. It will be like a great shifting of blocks. Krishnamurti taught me that. We're tight, Krish and ME.

Let's begin at the most important moment in the history of time, January 30, 9:00 p.m. Pacific time, the birth, death, and apotheosis of ME, Pearl. That was the point at which time stood still except for the interval between those identical dates and my immediate ascension into the realm that would become the glory that is ME. You might want to read that again. There will be a test. This followed shortly after January 21, National Squirrel Appreciation Day, which set up the conditions to make my arrival as auspicious as it was and ever will be. Blessed be, blessed ME. Squirrel Appreciation Day, or SAD, is a real thing. Look it up.

The best way to appreciate squirrels is to enjoy our antics from a distance and leave out fresh water all summer. Do not feed the squirrels. It makes us reliant on you as a food source. Sometimes we *are* reliant on you as a food source, in which case, step up to the plate, buckaroos, and fill it with nuts and honeydew.

But if you must feed all the squirrels, do not use peanuts. It just makes you look cheap. Rather, give us the more healthful walnuts in the shell. These can be frustratingly hard to get into so you'll want to gently crack each one just enough to preserve the challenge but still make access possible. Otherwise, it just daunts our giant spirits and nobody wants that. Granted this is a thankless, labor intensive and very expensive activity, so just do whatever you deem prudent.

We at ME Pearl put out the ultimate conventional calendar with fifteen months and 454 days and anchor dates that make sense to you. The purpose now is to alert you to dates and occasions that are lamentably missing from most commercial calendars. You're welcome. So, pull out your pen and your possum and let's start entering those essential mystical, magical, gastronomical, and astrological events that shape the days of our lives. If you don't yet have the genuine limited edition ME Pearl Ultimate Possum Calendar, you can follow along with any possum calendar you have hanging around. Most North American calendars have roughly the same number of months and weeks, give or take, but make no mistake, Big Squirrel is watching you, so keep up. The calendar cover reads, "Let's do better this year, shall we?" I bet we can all relate to that.

January

PAGE ONE, "BEGIN AGAIN." HERE WE HAVE A BRAND-NEW BABY possum entering the world looking absolutely terrified. Opossums, squirrels, birds, all semi-urban wildlife are suffering a great disadvantage on January 1 because it is preceded by New Year's Eve, and we know what that means, a night of explosive, relentless, and deafening fireworks. Wild mothers lose their wits and take off, leaving their young behind and often never finding their way home. Birds are spun off course, flying into buildings and trees, perishing on the spot. Animal shelters are packed to capacity with crazed domestic animals who have become hopelessly lost trying to escape the ear-piercing explosions, and those are the ones who survive. Surely there is a better way to celebrate a new year than by terrorizing our animals. Let's rethink this. Italy has.

And now for more important dates in January. January 4 is National Spaghetti Day! It's true. I mention this only because when people, such as yourself, write in to Pearl about problems with money, health, relationships, or lack thereof, she will often follow her sage advice with a spaghetti chaser. I don't know why. She knows things.

A brain-breaking amount of historical research has gone into "decoding" the first known calendar. Complex astronomical measurements have been calculated and recalculated. Seems the earliest calendars were lunar and made from sticks with notches adding up to between twenty-seven and thirty-three. And just who would be most interested in keeping track of what happens every twenty-seven to thirty-three days? Probably simpler than lofty male mathematical minds would have us believe. I propose that the female of your species created the first calendar after squirrels led the way by gnawing off and notching the best wood for the job. Behind every great invention is a squirrel waiting to be acknowledged.

There are more important dates in the course of recorded time. Dates requiring your mindful availability and involvement. Do we have to go in order? I don't want to. Besides it's not my order. This is not how I structured time, but I understand the need to work in segments you can grasp.

February

With the onset of February comes the realization that you've gotten off to a pretty rocky start. But never mind. Pearl understands and reminds you that it's never too late to begin again, again.

February 2 or thereabouts is Groundhog Day. Forget about Punxsutawney Phil. That poor baby doesn't know if he's coming or going. No, this is your opportunity to celebrate groundhogs in whatever fashion takes your fancy. You might invite a groundhog to lunch, or have a "take a groundhog to work" day, or simply make eye contact and say, "I see you. And I care." Oh, and vow to never play Whac-A-Mole again. Groundhogs feel a kinship with moles and such rude behavior really hurts their feelings, so don't do it.

February 2 is also Imbolc or Candlemas. Carried down from ancient times and traditions, Imbolc has been a day of initiation, of pledging loyalty to whatever you revere or hold sacred. By now, one assumes, Pearl de Wisdom to be your atman. These pledges are honored throughout the year and then renewed, or not, the following Imbolc. No one has not renewed their allegiance to Pearl.

February 14 is the day you let those special Valentine possums know how you feel by *not* giving them chocolate. This goes for dogs, cats, ferrets, parrots, pangolins, and anyone with an eating disorder, especially yourself. You know who you are. Instead, share a nice slice of vegan cheesecake. Tastes every bit as good as Vitameatavegemin and won't set off an inconvenient craving consuming everything in the path between you and more, more, *more*.

February 17 is Random Acts of Kindness Day. Of course, we feel that every day is Random Acts of Kindness Day and believe the Dalai Lama when he says, "Whenever possible, be kind. It is always possible."

March

MARCH 1 IS NATIONAL PIG DAY. REALLY, LOOK IT UP. FUN FACT: pigs are purportedly among the most intelligent animals, including dogs and dolphins. Also, pork is the most consumed animal protein in the world. What is wrong with these two fun facts? I want to speak directly to the pigs for a moment. What, in the name of Pearl are you using your brainpower for? Whatever it is, you need a shift in priorities. We know that you are social animals who communicate with each other all the time. So, organize, already! You could unionize, start a revolution, stage a coup, *something*. If you are waiting for humans to develop the moral and ethical integrity to treat you properly then you don't have the brains Goddess supposedly gave a pig. We at ME

Pearl usually believe that "tough love," like satanic possession and sleepwalking, is just an excuse. But in this case, *hello*—wake up and smell the bacon, Babe.

We do not like to be superstitious, not at all, and yet we are, which brings us to Mercury retrograde. You know how you feel after your first morning coffee or bloody Mary? That's Mercury direct. You know how you feel when on the verge of defenestrating yourself? That's Mercury retrograde. That's when everything stops going your way and it's best to just draw the blinds, lock the door, lay in a big supply of mochi, go to bed, pull the covers up over your head, and wait it out.

Mercury retrograde happens about three times a year, each lasting for approximately three weeks. During this time it is best if you don't go anywhere, don't do anything, don't say anything, don't sign anything, don't start anything. Don't marry anybody, don't divorce anybody and for Pearl's sake, don't conceive anybody. Why? There's no reason to go into detail but if you've seen *Rosemary's Baby* you get the gist. But enough of ME being a negative Nancy. If you must do any of these things, then remember: this is just superstitious nonsense. It doesn't mean anything. So fuhgeddaboudit it. You're gonna be fine. But if you're planning on donating to ME Pearl, sooner is better than later, if you catch my drift.

March 26 is National Something on a Stick Day, Vlad the Impaler's favorite. It's a real thing.

April

APRIL 15 IS WHEN AMERICANS RENDER UNTO SOME FALSE DEITY what rightfully belongs to Pearl and mark my barks and chatter, *there will be consequences!*

April 17 ushers in Lieldienas, a Latvian spring equinox event, celebrating the victory of light over darkness. But "victory over" implies dominance and when it comes to light and dark that's just dumb. Don't be dumb.

April 20 is considered by some to be Smoke Cannabis Day. Amateurs.

Easter, Ishtar, Ostara, Eostre, Goddess of Spring, Freshness, Light. Your Pearlie Mae is here shaking her head in puzzlement and perplexity. How and why have the origins of what you call Easter become so muddled and mucked up? Naturally, it is not my fault. Nothing is. But I magnanimously take responsibility for clarifying everything for you. After all, who else is qualified to do it? Allow ME to squirrelsplain. All that imagery overrun with rabbitry is ridiculous. There was never a rabbit. There was only ever a squirrel. THE squirrel. ME squirrel. Easter isn't Christian or Pagan; it's pure Pearlian, through and through.

Recreated in retrospect, the holiday is now Pearlia, a time of Pearlian resplendence, of celebrating the light within ME. Do not be discouraged.There will be ample opportunity to dance in my darkness come the Autumnal Equinox. But today, go out and find as many eggs as you can and return them to the chickens. This is a day to look at everything you took, and put it back.

May

MAY 1, MAY DAY! BELTANE. A DAY TO REJOICE IN THE SPLENDOR that is you by dancing around a decorated maypole with somebody special. You're special.

Marriage. People love weddings. Why? Is it because it brings our villages closer together? And they cry. I cried at Georgette's wedding but only because she was thinking of something other than ME for an instant, poising our world on the brink of collapse.

But then her betrothed became besotted with ME and all was right with the world. But "Marry in May, rue the day," is an ancient saying with a valid basis.

Donkeys are amorous in May. So are pigs and goats and sheep and cattle and lemurs. Hence the festival of Lemuria in ancient Rome. Do you really want to get married while livestock are getting it on? They say it's not a competition but it sort of is. How will your solemn vows hold focus while pigs are squealing, "Do it for me, Daddy!"

Speaking of which, Orthodox porcine morning prayer: Thank you, God, for not making me a clean animal.

June

June 22. Summer Solstice or Midsummer . . . the turning point of the year, the halfway mark. How ya doin'? Any of those resolutions still in play? Never mind. Pearl loves you. It's Litha, a holiday of gratitude for light and life. At Litha, adherents note the full abundance of nature at the point of midsummer. Traditionally, fresh fruits and vegetables are the main course at shared meals, and bonfires are lit to pay homage to the power of the sun. Also, if you've been planning a plunge into Shakespeare, *A Midsummer Night's Dream* may be your most accessible portal. Only one fatal flaw, no squirrels.

July

July 4. Shall we revisit fireworks? Opossums, squirrels, birds, all semi-urban wildlife are likely to suffer greatly on July 4 and the surrounding week because bozos like to make boom boom. Days and nights of relentless, and deafening, fireworks. Wild mothers lose their wits and take off, leaving their young behind and often never finding their way home. Birds are spun off course, flying into buildings and trees, breaking their necks, and perishing on the spot. Animal shelters are packed to capacity with crazed domestic animals who have become hopelessly lost trying to escape the ear-piercing explosions, and those are the ones who survive. Surely there is a better way to celebrate independence than by terrorizing our "best friends."

August

AUGUST 1, LUGHNASADH, A HOLIDAY WHERE WE EXPRESS GRATI-tude that we are not expected to speak Gaelic. And to Gaia, Mother Earth, for bread. And who isn't grateful for bread? Not just the baguette or Bavarian pumpernickel or even the wonder that was Wonder Bread, but rather the very essence of bread, including crackers and biscuits. It harkens back to a day when no one was gluten intolerant.

September

SEPTEMBER 21. AUTUMN EQUINOX OR MABON. AS PROMISED, YOU may now dance the darkness that is ME. Then sit one out and celebrate a true Thanksgiving: no Native Americans, no Pilgrims, and not a turkey in sight. Gather in the gifts of the earth, hearty foods like gourds, pumpkins, grapes, and apples. Modern Mabon celebrations are a time to give thanks for the abundance of Mother Earth—both literally and spiritually. This is the second harvest. Lughnasadh was the first. Go ahead, read that out loud. It's also a good time to reflect on the Wheel of the Year, recognizing your successes and letting go of the things that did not serve you during the past twelve months.

October

OCTOBER 31. HALLOWEEN, ALL HALLOWS EVE, SAMHAIN. THAT time when the veil between the worlds is thinnest and we honor our departed ancestors and personal heroes and sheroes. It would be advisable to start now so you'll be prepared when the time comes. Get out a piece of parchment and a calligraphy pen with a Brause Steno 361 nib, more commonly known as the Blue Pumpkin. Or thumb it into a smart phone, if you must. You could also use a quill dipped in blood, preferably your own. A bold choice.

Now make a list of everyone who matters to you or who needs your prayerful remembrance. Just jot down whoever comes to mind: deceased animal companions, historical figures, mentors in any discipline, even celebrities. Who isn't still pained by the passing of Agnes Moorehead, for example?

Now take a platter of homemade sweetmeats, popcorn will do in a pinch, and for every name on your list, toss a pastry or kernel onto the roof at witching hour. You'll probably have to go outdoors to do this. Along with each "event," check in with the entity you've summoned and let them know why they are important to you. Remember, this may be the most attention they've had all century so make it good.

But—who else may partake of these ritual goodies? Who, other than dead S.O.s, may be visiting your rooftop? No, not jolly ol' St. Nick. There. Yes. Exactly! Birds, roof rats, raccoons, squirrels, possums, rabbits . . . and what will happen when—not if, *when*—they ingest all that refined sugar, corn syrup, sodium, saturated fat, and Red Dye 40? That's right, hyperglycemia and ADHD, to say nothing of the 10 percent likely to develop an addiction. Is that what you want? What's the matter with you? Shame on you. Instead, we recommend your Samhain platter be made up of organic berries, veggies, nuts and seeds, hummus, wheatgrass, and seaweed. It just makes sense and I'm sure your dead loved ones will thank you. And may someone someday remember you with love and legumes.

Or would you rather celebrate Satan's birthday by dressing up and threatening your neighbors? TRICK OR TREAT?! It's another approach. In case you don't know, the opossum's favorite treat is:

> Fillet of a fenny snake,
>
> In the cauldron boil and bake;
>
> Eye of newt and toe of frog,
>
> Wool of bat and tongue of dog,
>
> Adder's fork, and blind-worm's sting,
>
> Lizard's leg, and howlet's wing,

For a charm of powerful trouble,

Like a hell-broth boil and bubble.[21]

Whereas, their favorite trick is to poop on the stoop, slap the door with their tail, then waddle off and hide in the bushes. It never gets old. Once again, let me draw your attention to the elephant in the book. Seems like Mr. Elephant is acting out a lot lately. Where is the angel dust when you really need it? If you don't know, the designer drug called angel dust was designed as a tranquilizer for elephants. So, if you're still using it (like you, Linda Sherwood), think about it.

Hey, peeps, do you know about elephant dung stationary and other paper products? Well, you should. Here is a:

Pachyderm PSA

Now I know that none of you would ever buy products made of ivory. This is just hideously compromising to an elephant and you would never do it. In fact, if you have a piano with ivory keys you just defenestrate that right now. I mean it. Go ahead, defenestrate! Toss that atrocity of a Steinway out the window. There now. Feel better? You will, because there is an ethical way to satisfy that craving we all feel for elephant essence.

Elephant Poop Paper Products. You can now purchase Elephant Poop greeting cards, elephant poop address books, personal journals,

---

21 *Macbeth*, act 4, scene 1, William Shakespeare

guest registers, and, just think, you can even have your wedding album and baby book made out of elephant poop. Elephant Poop Paper Products make the perfect gift for every occasion. And the best part? The elephant never misses it.

One of the more interesting Darwin Awards went to an elephant keeper who was martyred relieving his charge of a stubborn case of constipation.

As we all know by now, the vast majority of opossums belong outside. If you see one there, leave it there. . . . If you come across an ill, injured, or orphaned opossum, contact a professional wildlife rehabber immediately. If, after all that, you're still left with a possum or two, become a staunch advocate for respecting and protecting the dignity of all wildlife. Sure, dress 'em up, but stick with Brooks Brothers and J.Crew. Lady opossums? Vera Wang all the way.

November

NOVEMBER IS THE OFFICIAL NORTH AMERICAN TIME OF Thanksgiving, and I don't mind slaving over a hot stove to show loved ones how thankful I am to have them in my life, because nothin' says lovin' like pumpkin from the oven. Each pie touched with love. I put a thumb print and the possum puts a pawprint in the center of each pie. Then I wrap each pie in traditional blue lace. Each year we make one for poor cousin Whatshisname in the home. I don't think they ever did give him a name, but we're going to give him a pie. And there's always one for Clayton, the mailman, who was such a good sport about that incident involving our German Guard Opossum. Of course, a pie cannot replace a thumb, but we try. We use an old family recipe to give the personal touch to those who matter. Sometimes people are fooled by the Sara Lee protective packaging. You should get little stickers that read, "Compliments of . . . ." If you don't know what to note after that, just write, "ME Pearl, donations welcome." Be sure there is plenty of pie left for you and the possums and plenty of nitrous oxide in cans of nondairy whipped cream.

I don't often cook but when I do, I use a sturdy yet stylish large-pocketed ME Pearl apron from our online store. And I would be remiss not to mention once again that we also have our signature calendar waiting for you. What better holiday gift for your weird friends or your weird self? You'll notice that November's eerily disconcerting image and sentiment of our beloved leader is the same as on this apron. Coincidental synchronicity? I think not. I like to read books in the bathtub so we usually make several pies for our very forgiving librarian, Mrs. Titlebaum.

November is also the month when friends and families get together to give thanks for their many blessings and for each other. And what better way to celebrate Turkey Day than by contacting a farm animal sanctuary and adopting a turkey, just for the irony of it. I know what you're thinking, but you're wrong.

You don't actually have to bring the turkey into your home. No. You simply accept financial responsibility for the care of that turkey for the rest of its natural life. You may even get to name it! Cool, right?

And if you are fortunate enough to be invited by family or friends to a special holiday gathering, two tips: don't arrive drunk and don't leave through the bathroom window.

December

DECEMBER 21. WINTER SOLSTICE OR YULE. HERE IT'S FINE TO celebrate as you normally would this time of year. As joyous and jubilant as we humans feel during this Yule season of love and celebration, these uplifted feelings do not always translate to our beloved companion animals and the wildlife in our care. Many of them simply don't love Jesus, particularly, or appreciate the gnostic significance of the Winter Solstice, or all the hoopla over Holofernes's head for Hanukkah.

All our happy music and unbridled laughter may serve to restimulate some unknown puppy, kitten, joey, or cubhood trauma, leading to depression, despair, and then the unspeakable. If you don't want your house littered with dead animals by the first of the year, let me share a few cheery suggestions for staving off misery.

Festive holiday sweaters are sure to raise spirits high. Ask Gramma to crochet a bunch if she's the type. Otherwise, it's off to the marsupial supply outlet to take advantage of those "once-a-year-gotta-be-crazy" holiday specials you've all been waiting for. The larger marsupial supply outlets will feature a wide array of festive stylish clothing in a range of colors and sizes for all of your favorite wildlife species.

Humorous headgear is a must. Putting reindeer antlers on a mule deer is especially good for a chuckle. And what opossum can resist vegan eggnog? I defy you to find any species of wildlife who isn't simply crazy for vegan eggnog. In fact, if you're looking for some real holiday fun you might stage your own vegan eggnog comparison taste test challenge. Go into the woods with biodegradably packaged samples of rice, almond, coconut, oat, and soy eggnog and let the fun begin. Just fling those packets about and see who comes running.

With the right spin that activity could replace hunting. Another word to hunters: "Vengeance is mine," sayeth the squirrel.

If you decide to decorate a tree inside your house you gotta know that, to animals, it just looks like a giant toy rack and whatever happens is on you.

Sure, you're going to want all of your three- and four-legged friends to join in the celebrations and it's fine to let them dress up, bake cookies, open presents, play the piano, etc., but otherwise, keep their eating and exercise routines on track.

Remember that munching on mistletoe, holly, and poinsettia can be toxic for both you and your animals, so don't do it. Just don't! No. But, if you must, here is the number for poison control: 888-426-4435.

In this season of joy and giving, good will to all, it's likely that many of you will become debilitatingly depressed, much like we do, here at ME Pearl (Enterprises). So how do we cope? Gingerbread with a generous drizzle of lemon glaze.

This brings us to the end of the year, the time of closure and reckoning. But with the ME Pearl calendar you get three extra months to procrastinate plus the opportunity to buy next year's calendar at a whopping discount, possibly.

And finally, on the back, the fundamental reminder that "it's all gonna be OK." Because "Pearl loves you, in spite of everything." So be of good cheer, hold on tight, and try not to fall off your Wheel of the Year.

Note: You will be ever so much happier if you simply give in and go with the revolutions and the ebb and the flow of the earth and the oceans.

Joining the Cult of Pearl, or The Squirrel Made Me Do It

IF YOU ARE ON THE CUSP OF JOINING THE COSMIC CULT OF PEARL de Wisdom, Goddess of the Multiverse, and then some, here may be the deciding factor. Our religion comes with SQUIRRELS: angel squirrels and daemon squirrels and all the in-between 'em squirrels.

For example: Sometimes others, when looking at you, may see the squirrelly little angels and daemons you carry, whereas you may have no clue, no idea how much these little shoulder pads hold sway over your every attitude and action.

Did you hear the ancient Cherokee tale about the two squirrels sitting on the shoulders of some well-seasoned Caucasian chick? Well, they are and they're engaged in a great battle. One is a daemon. He is anger and arrogance, brutality, cruelty, destruction, envy, false pride, lies, resentment, guilt, regret, and greed. What a bad squirrel. That baby is a handful!

The other is good. She is benevolence, compassion, empathy, goodwill, honor, joy, peace, love, truth, and kindness. She can be a bit hard to take, sometimes. The same fight is going on inside you . . . unless it's not, in which case you are one lucky ducky, which reminds me of a clarifying quote from whence I don't recall.

> I envy people who have all their ducks in a row. I don't have ducks. I only have squirrels, and they're all drunk.

So, which squirrel will win? Supposedly it's the one you feed. However, have you ever felt that you've lost track of who you're feeding, of who is a daemon and who is an angel? Or whether angels and daemons even exist? Now we're talkin'! Let's say that, whether for good or for ill or for pure entertainment, you find yourself having done something you'd rather not account for. Who hasn't? That's when we at ME Pearl come to your rescue. That's right. We have your back, babe. Now you, along with the vast majority of our loyal fans and followers, know to go to our web store and purchase our favorite slogan, TSMMDI: The Squirrel Made Me Do It. For just . . . whatever the market will bear, you can have your own sticky banner excuse for whatever transgression floats your boat. Just affix it to whatever requires an explanation or simply slap it across your chest as one big mea culpa. You can wear your banner with, maybe not pride, exactly, but with conviction.

So, do angel and daemon squirrels really exist? Decide for yourself. In either case, elephants exist and there is one trumpeting around this book right now reminding us that the vast majority of squirrels belong outside. When you see them there, enjoy the antics and leave them alone. If you come across an ill, injured, or orphaned squirrel, contact a professional wildlife rehabilitator immediately. If, after all that, you are still left with a squirrel, consider that it may not be a squirrel at all. It may be a vision of the great divine Pearl de Wisdom, herself.

So, if you are a rodent lover between religions, recently aware of the squirrel-shaped hole in your soul, come join us and partake in the paradise that is Pearl. (Oh, people, people, friends even, please know that I, Georgette Spelvin, would never drool this drivel, deliver this dreck if it were not for the humiliating fact that . . . .

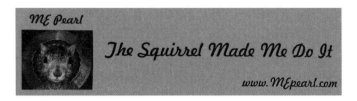

The Seven Deadly Virtues by Pearl

ARE YOU SICK TO DEATH OF THE SEVEN DEADLY SINS? BEEN THERE, done that? I know I am. So, for a change of pace, let's explore that virgin territory of untrod paths and unrealized opportunities: the hidden world of virtue, usually reserved for reformed drunks (don't get ME started) and dullards . . . . Release your seatbelts, it's gonna be a meh ride.

Pagans have no set rules against premarital sex, homosexuality, masturbation, or nudity. However, sex is viewed as the generative force in nature and is seen by most pagans as something utterly sacred. The physical act of love is to be approached with great respect and responsibility. While premarital sex is not forbidden, adultery may violate a sacred trust between man and woman (or squirrel), unless parties stipulate otherwise. Okay, you decide. But, let's make one thing perfectly clear:

Bestiality from the Beast's POV

YUCK! EWW, BLACH, PTHEWY, UH-UH.

CHASTITY. The word derives from the Latin *castitas,* the abstract form of *castus,* which originally meant a pure state of conformity with the Greco-Roman religion. (Really?!) As the etymological link suggests, castigation, chastisement, and in the extreme case, even castration originally relate to the use of harsh means to preserve or restore this state of purity. This meaning is preserved fully in the parallel term "chastening." Sound good?

TEMPERANCE. Don't wanna, can't make ME.

CHARITY. This one is more from you to ME. But don't think of it as charity. It would be properly considered tithing, or tribute. Bring it on!

PERSEVERANCE. I can't emphasize this enough: you don't have to if you don't want to. Always ask yourself, *Will this lead to chocolate?* If the answer is *Yes*, do something else, because you know what eating chocolate does to you: the depression, the misery, the self-hatred, the tears and surliness, the stained bathrobe, the broken promises, the canceled dates, failed deadlines, missed appointments, lost opportunities, reduced expectations, revised goals, and the realization that you'll always be alone. Don't do it.

PATIENCE. Moving on.

KINDNESS. I believe in this more than anything. But it's kind of theoretical.

HUMILITY. Always best in my presence and inevitable when thinking of ME. Do you regularly ask yourself, *What would Pearl do?* Why not? Try it. By the way, the answer to the question "What would Pearl do?" is "Be kind." It may not be true but it is the right answer.

Pearlestine Prophesies

FIRST INSIGHT
I AM ARCHETYPE.
Not you, this has nothing to do with you. *I* am Archetype,
ME, Pearl.

I am the Missing Archetype. Sort of like the missing link only
better. Newly emerged and yet part of your collective unconscious
since Time Imodium.

Archetypal ME

SECOND INSIGHT

You *can* take it with you. Everything you possess turns astral and comes over when you croak. So pay attention to what you stash and trash. It matters. Matter doesn't matter but essence is everything.

THIRD INSIGHT

We continue to age over here. But it's not as you would expect from earthly experience. The aging process is not contingent on time. Changes are the accumulation of choices and experiences and judgments and influences and friends and lovers and accidents, etc. It has nothing to do with the body breaking down because it doesn't. But it does keep changing and, in most cases, you can easily tell by looking how long a being has been boppin' about, except in the case of Buddhists and porpoises and Shar-Peis and anything Finlandian.

FOURTH INSIGHT
You're not ready yet.

FIFTH INSIGHT
It is not coincidence that you now have need of the very item you recently discarded. It is the law of cause and effect. It is *because* you threw it out that the need for it arose, so be of good cheer and do not berate yourself for lack of foresight. Had you not rid yourself of the item, you would have no need for it now and it would still be cluttering your life.

SIXTH INSIGHT
Early Life:

a. When in doubt, don't.
b. Whatever you are pretending to be, you probably are.
c. What others are saying about you is probably true.

Later Life:

a. When in doubt, go ahead. Let's see what happens.
b. Whatever you are pretending to be, stop it.
c. What others are saying about you is irrelevant.

SEVENTH INSIGHT

That third party in your mind isn't real.

EIGHTH INSIGHT

In response to the question: Is Earth the only location in our galaxy where life exists? If not, how far is the closest? The closest location is Etherea and it's less than a breath away. Anybody who was anybody is here and can see and influence everything you do and think. Like now.

Oh, stop showing off. It may take you a while to get used to this idea and relax. But you will. Those activities that embarrass you most tend to bore us to distraction. But most of us retain an avid interest in food and, as often as not, your food choices are not entirely your own.

As for other locations, sure. Inner-, inter-, and extra-galaxy. But it's always the same beings being recycled and repurposed hither, thither and yon. There is nobody new under whatever sun happens to be out or not.

Ninth Insight

Do not debate the form when you crave the content.

Extra Insight

Notice what people have too much of and at gift giving time give them that. It's what they like.

Another Extra Insight

Do not be afraid of aging. Although not immediately apparent, there are multitudinous perks.

Quick Tip

When engaged in an argument or heated debate, throw in a word your adversary does not understand. You don't have to understand it either. In fact, it's best if it's not a real word at all. This works especially well if your opponent is too proud to admit they don't know the word. It will really throw them off their game. You're welcome.

Another Quick Tip

Never underestimate anyone with a Swiss Army Knife.

The Secret to Everlasting Happiness by Pearl

DRUGS—BUT I DON'T ADVISE THEM. THE NEXT BEST THING TO EVER-lasting happiness is even better. Having enough. And you do, or you wouldn't have put out money on a book like this or spent the time to read it. But having enough isn't enough. You must know to the bone marrow that you do. Observe squirrels. We are the happiest creatures in creation. Of course, we hoard, don't we, so never mind. Bad example. Just erase that from your mind. Pretend I didn't say it. Most people have trouble truly believing that they have enough. And that is why I, Pearl de Wisdom, have developed a cult.

If you join my cult, you will join the elite. You will feel superior to others, and that's always a warm fuzzy. But, best of all, you will discover that you have *more* than enough. And that's why I, your beloved leader, have devised an easy means of direct donation: patreon.com/MEpearl. It's a bit like medieval bloodletting. You keep giving to ME until you feel better. That's when you know to stop. Sound good? Good.

Your Beloved Leader

To Be or Not to Be . . . a Squirrel
by Georgette

AS YOU HAVE SURMISED BY NOW, I ADORE POSSUMS! THEY ARE SO pure. After seventy million years, I kid you not, fossils of possums are found next to fossils of dinosaurs, and they have remained innocent. They are touchingly simple, without guile. And let's face it, they're funny! I have been writing about and videoing possums for well over a decade because possums are funny, and metaphorical, and I love them.

But would I want to be a possum? No. Urban, suburban, or wild, the life of the possum is hard. Now I do believe in reincarnation. I know, many of you are thinking, *That's crazy. I know better than that. Only a marginalized nut would believe something like that.* OK, maybe, but consider this; two-thirds of the world believes this way. That's a majority. And most of these people meditate hours a day seeking only what's real, looking for the truth. And this is what they come back with; the transmigration of souls. Just sayin'. And animals have souls. Clearly. There are ample examples of animals putting themselves at risk for the benefit of others. Plus, we can see them dreaming.

So reincarnation or transmigration of souls includes animals. I don't see it as a hierarchy, just a broadening of experience. I would never make a value judgment on an opossum and neither should you. Do I want to be an opossum? No. But a squirrel . . . "'tis a consummation devoutly to be wished."[22] Birds fly and that must be wonderful. But squirrels dance through the sky, bounding through treetops in a state of absolute joy. Squirrels were made for joy. It's their nature.

I wouldn't want to be an urban squirrel, too much human interference. Nor a captive squirrel, however benevolent the captor. Squirrels are meant to live free. Anything less is frustrating. Wouldn't want to be a squirrel in North Dakota. Brrrrr.

But a squirrel in a forest in a temperate clime. Oh wow! And suppose at some point you do get plucked out of the air by a raptor, or swallowed whole by a serpent . . . bummer . . . oh yeah, big bummer

---

22 *Hamlet*, act 3, scene 1, William Shakespeare.

. . . but, for those few years of exhilaration, worth it, so worth it. In fact, I expect I've already been a squirrel. How else to explain this close connection, this understanding? Been there, done that, loved it!

And, now for *you*. Let's think about *you*. What are you drawn to, inspired by, connected with that seemingly has no explanation, but it's deep and it's true and it's yours? If you can think of something, let me know on our website. I'll be fascinated.

The State of the World by Pearl

MOST PEOPLE BELIEVE THAT THE WORLD HAS A LOT OF PROBLEMS. In fact, the world has only one problem. Can you guess? Porcupines. More on that in our next book, *Pearls Before Swine*, no offense.

In Closing by Georgette

HOW CAN YOU HELP?

Look up the numbers of your veterinarian, after-hours emergency veterinarian, local animal shelter, and wildlife rehabilitation center and sanctuary, and enter them into your smart phone.

Volunteer at local wildlife centers and sanctuaries. "Never forget it's a wild animal" is a phrase that is often used to suggest that the animal may turn on you and/or hurt you. This may be true, but the point is more nuanced and far-reaching. This animal, however habituated, has an inner life with needs and instincts your mind is incapable of comprehending. However much you may love or learn about them, they will never be your pet, your baby, your buddy. They are forever other, to be respected, observed, and marveled at.

Commentary by Pearl

Yeah, yeah, yeah, blah, blah, blah—just send ME money, gift certificates, cards, cashier's checks, and gifts, c/o Apollo Publishers. Do NOT send ME your children. I don't want them either.

Be sure to watch ME and the others on our YouTube channel, MEpearlA, and hustle! You are already way far behind. Just think where you could be today if only you had started watching and lucubrating back in 2010. Don't, it will break your brain. Always remember Pearl Loves You. And You Love Pearl. And that is the secret of the Multiverse. Apply it to everything.

You're welcome.

PART FIVE

Ask Pearl

Early Pearlie

Dear Pearl,

I feel like all these people need my help, especially my boyfriend, all the time. I get so irritated that I pretend I don't understand sometimes to avoid helping them but then I feel terrible after. How can I be more comfortable without being rude?
Marcia

Pearl says:

Marcia, hey! Rude is an art form. Learn it.

Root out the selfish ones. Give in to the lunatic you really are and scare the losers away. Some folks make you feel that you should be smaller than you really are.

Nobody is responsible for how much space they naturally take up. It just is. Do not be ashamed if you take up a lot.

Next time some whiney-whiney wants something you don't feel like giving, throw them out the window . . . and their little dog too—just kidding. *Never throw an animal out the window.* It's OK to throw humans out the window, because they have nine lives and always land on their feet. Go ahead, try it. You'll see.

We have been happy to offer you these pearls of wisdom. Good luck to you.

Dear Pearl,

What are your plans for taking over the world? I might be able to help you on that rocky road to fascism . . . . ALL HAIL MEPEARL.

Pearl says:

You don't expect ME to just tell you my plans, do you? I'm not Pearl de *Wisdom* for nothing!

Dear Pearlie,

I threw my boyfriend out like you said. I should move on—but I can't. I think it's because I just cannot believe it's over. Maybe I could just pretend he's dead, but then I'll be sad and that's no good. He was my best friend. I just don't know if this is the best thing for either of us.

Pearl says:

Marcia, Marcia, Marcia . . . . Relationships never die. You can't kill them with a sledgehammer. You can't kill them with a guillotine or a poison ring or an asp.

You can't drop a piano on them or hit them upside the head with an anvil or lock them in a freezer or throw them into oncoming traffic. You cannot kill a relationship with a laser gun or a silver bullet. You can't stab a relationship to death or run over it with a tractor or push it off a cliff. You cannot tie it to a train track or drown it in a swimming pool or suffocate it with a big pillow or a plastic baggie. You cannot scare a relationship to death or surprise it with a school of sharks or bury it in a hill of red ants. You cannot blow it to smithereens with high-powered explosives or asphyxiate it with poison gas or dispatch it with an axe or a blowtorch or an electric chainsaw. A stampede of wild cattle will not kill a relationship. You cannot anaphylactic shock it to death or kill it with a tommy gun or by throwing a toaster into a therapist's office. Poison darts won't work any more than dropping it into a mire of quicksand. A relationship will not die of old age or neglect or a rusty stake through its heart. You cannot give it a stomach parasite or sponge brain or wring its neck or kill it with a trash compactor. A relationship cannot even commit suicide. Relationships never die, but they do transform sometimes. Boyfriend could show up as your special needs granddaughter on Mars or your puppy. You and boyfriend may decide to take separate vacations for maybe a fortnight or a couple of lifetimes. It's not over until it's over, Marcia, and it's never over. So relax.

Dear Pearl,

Oh Pearlie Mae, you are wise. And I don't want to kill it or wish death on it. It is what it is.

Thanks,
Marcia

Pearl says:

Ah, oui, Marcia. *C'est vrai. C'est bien vrai. J'ais raison, tout le temps.*

La Pearl de Sagesse

Dear Pearl,

I am very frustrated. The two-leggers in my neighborhood drive fast and don't pay attention to squirrels in the street. I have young ones and need help.

Pearl says:

Yes, yes, this can be very frustrating, but you will be happy to learn that the answer is simple. Teach your young ones to run down the street in a zig-zaggy motion. That will confuse the giant rolling Peep shells. This has been a very popular technique with many astral squirrels of my acquaintance.

Hi Mrs. Pearl,

I have read your stories and watched your videos, and I think I am in love with you. I want to be your Latin lover. I am forty years old, from Florida, and I want to please you and make you mine. I want to send pictures, but I am shy. I will send some if you are interested, in the nude if you want. I am willing to go to great lengths to pleasure your body in every way.

Your friend,

J

Pearl says:

Hi J,

First things first—

Are you a squirrel?
–Pearl the Particular

Dear Pearl,

Pearl of my life, I am a raccoon who lives in Seattle. You have a very hairy tail, and luxurious. My wish is to be with you, and to have a child, half squirrel, half raccoon. I am thinking of your love and your caresses. I have a lot of love in my little heart, and it is all yours. My love, my Pearl, come to me here in Seattle, and we will make love to the jungle with nature.

–Joseph the Raccoon

Pearl says:

Here's the problem, J: I'm dead.

–Pearl the Passed Over

Dear Pearl,

I used to think aging would be fun. Now I'm not so sure. Too many "senior moments." Words fly out of brain. Brain has tantrum. Words return when they're no longer appropriate. Damn words. Damn brain. Damn aging. How do *you* cope?

Pearl says:

Pearl knows your pain. Ah oui. In my business *le bon mot* is all important and when it flies out of the brain, the brain does, indeed, "have tantrum." But Pearl of Problem Solving has found a solution: when my brain loses a desired word, I simply think of what I wish to say in Portuguese and then do so. For example: *Isto é-ME, Pérola Portuguesa, ostentando. Não é enchidos com admiração e maravilha?* See? Works like a charm every time. Try it.

As for aging, I coped by croaking at the end of my eleventh year. Here, let ME offer you a profound insight into the afterlife. We continue to age over here, but it's not as you would expect from earthly experience. The aging process is not contingent on time. Changes are the accumulation of choices and experiences and judgments and influences and friends and lovers and accidents, etc.

It has nothing to do with the body breaking down because it doesn't, but it does keep changing.

Dear Pearl,

Recent on-and-off viewing of the Vancouver Olympics has awakened a dream that will not die, and it haunts me. A dear friend and I have long intended to win gold medals for ice dancing at an Olympics when we get around to it, and I am crushed at the thought that it will now be another four years before this is possible. Despite obvious courage and spiritual strength, the two of us are exactly the sort of unlikely long shots who always endear themselves to viewers—we are both in our seventh decades, I have two fused vertebrae and a crushed sciatic nerve, and my friend has two artificial hips. Neither of us has ever skated competitively (or, in my case, skated at all), and we are both quite busy with other things a lot of the time. However, as our culture teaches us, it is the dream that counts, and we are already gold medalists at dreaming. Please help me chart out the most efficient route possible to the achievement of this goal, preferably in a way that would involve as little discomfort as possible—to go directly to the podium and the medals ceremony would be optimal.

Sincerely,

My Dream Is Your Command

Pearl says:

Dear MDIYC,

Your challenge intrigues the Pearl. Hmm. Yes. Yes, Pearl de Wisdom can help you realize your dream. Ah oui, bien sur.

I am the most efficient route possible to achievement of this goal. Let ME explain. What would take your act over the top is ME, a three-legged squirrel in a formfitting dance dress and one shiny little skate.

Let's represent Morocco, just for fun.

OK, so here's the vision: You two hold hands and glide carefully across the ice to the center of the rink then *surprise*, I pop out from under the skirt of your partner's costume. The crowd will gasp, believe you ME. I will then climb up your partner's still but colorfully bedecked torso and leap off her head into a triple axel Lutz cantilever, culminating in a Besti squat. Can you see it? I grew up listening to the Village Stompers strumming "Tie Me Kangaroo Down, Sport" and it will cheer me to have the emotional support of amplified banjos strumming through the stadium. You too?

You then lean over pointing down with your thumb, which I will use as a push-off point to gain momentum for multiple one-legged crossovers around your stationary body, ending in a death-spiral spin. Can you see it?

Then you straighten up (take your time, they will be looking at ME). You and your partner now stand side by side, silent and still (note how Pearl of Compassion looks after your deteriorating corporal containers) while I do combination camel jumps from one to the other, squeeze in a quick Jackson Haines spin under your left arm and drop into a shoot-the-duck. Can you see it?

I shall make my skate a mirror so you can check your makeup as the blade whizzes past your face from every possible direction, then round and round and round and round and round . . . .

As the audience holds its collective breath, I shall risk a one-legged swizzle sheep jump through the double ring of fire, created by you and your partner making slow overlapping circles while holding burning cigarette lighters.

Then, after executing a delightfully unexpected Ina Bauer hydroblading cherry flip, we'll gear up for our grand finale.

As the last chords of the dueling banjos stop, the two of you shall face each other touching foreheads, thus forming a human pyramid atop of which I shall dazzle the crowd with a dizzying variation of my signature move: the flying ME Pearl vertical squirrelly-whirl aerial super spin, named after ME, Pearl. *Can you see it?*

As the roar of appreciation finally subsides, we shall confidently make our way to the kiss-and-cry area awaiting our unanimous 10s and ultimately the undisputed gold.

The only thing that could possibly go wrong is the outside chance that the judges may lack the imagination to connect with the astral plane on which I operate. In other words, they may not see ME.

That could result in your routine appearing a wee bit lackluster, but the burning cigarette lighters are a bright and unusual touch. Fire always takes focus. You might consider lighting your partner's headdress as a last resort.

Oh boy, oh boy, oh boy! Pearl of the Dance is all happy and excited now. I don't think we'll need to rehearse, do you?

Meet you guys at the Olympics. You sign in or whatever it is you have to do to register.

Dear Pearl,

There are many different kinds of squirrels: red, pine, fox, eastern gray, western gray, rock, flying, ground and so on . . . . What kind of squirrel are you?

Pearl says:

Who wants to know?

Dear Pearl,

Any wisdom concerning the fact that life passes *much too quickly*? It used to be a somewhat leisurely activity. Now there's barely time to look up at the sky . . . .

–R. R.

Pearl says:

Hello R. R.,

Life actually passes *very slowly* when you have one leg and live in a cage. But I don't recommend it.

You have plenty of time to do anything you want, just not everything you want. Besides, this life is just a drop in a very big, overflowing bucket. You go to sleep, you wake up. You get thrown under a bus, you wake up. You get cannibalized by another aboriginal, you wake up. And so on.

Pearl of Wisdom is beginning to really like you, new friend. In fact, I like you so much that I want to encourage you to start thinking seriously about joining me. I can assure you that most of the fun is on this side, but, of course, this is coming from someone who, again, had one leg and lived in a cage.

Yes, yes, Pearl of Wisdom embraces inconsistencies and wants to embrace you. Come into these furry little *brazos*, *mi amiga*. C'mon, R. R., come join the party! You know you want to.

Dear Pearlie,

Your answer was duly received and I too feel close and loving. Actually, I'll see you soon at the rate our world is turning, and without any messy debris from inept suicide attempts. By the way, I thought you had three legs. Can't wait to compare notes with you when I arrive. But watch out for the leopards . . . .

–R. R.

Pearl says:

Hey! Those leopards better watch out for ME! What leopards? Seriously. Leopards? Where?
Blessings,
Pearl the Paralyzed

P.S. More on arms and legs later. Bottom line, Pearl sets the standard. Two arms, one leg. All else is vanity and excess. Seriously, tell ME about the leopards. I'm not kidding around.

Dear Pearl,

Pink Mama needs your wisdom. My friend, Debbie, has given me an amazing gift. She expended so much time and effort and expertise to give me something I really want. She built me an incredible professional website with multiple bells and whistles and it's *soooo* superior to the one I constructed.

I'm awed. I'm embarrassed. I don't know how to thank her enough. I have no idea how to repay her for this extreme generosity. What should I say? What can I give her? What can I do to show her how much this means to me? I feel I don't deserve it.

Pearl says:

Hey, Pink Mama, a.k.a. Georgette,

You *don't* deserve it. It isn't for you. It's for ME. She created this website for ME. The Debster and I are really tight and it's only natural that she would whip up a little something to express her appreciation of ME. In fact, I was wondering what took her so long. Aunt Debbie knows I'm too valuable, too important, too iconic for that crap you created. So get over yourself and relax. The Pearl needs a clear channel.

Hi Pearl,

My partner and I are new fans. We like how you think but you have divided us about money.

I want to send you something and Astrid says I'm crazy. We have a joint account and have to agree on these things. Will you make Astrid see that it's OK to do this?

We may have some relationship issues to ask you about later.
Thanks, Squirrely.

Jacquelyn

Pearl says:

Dear Jacquelyn,

The Pearl does not seek to convince, persuade, or cajole. Pearl of Plenty simply allows. I have provided the means through which all may give to ME that which pleases them. I am good. You are blessed. Send money.

Dear Ms. de Wisdom,

With all due respect, I don't see why you need money and gifts if you are dead.
Astrid

Pearl says:

Ah, poor Astrid,

You think in terms of need, my friend, and that keeps you poor. Pearl of Getting lives in a world of desire. I desire money and gifts and that makes it right for ME to receive them. It's so simple, really. Just release and relax and go with the flow. In this case the flow is from you to ME. From you to ME. My open arms are here to receive. It's easy, Astrid. Just let go. You're welcome.

Pearl of MINE, all MINE.

Dear Pearl,

So, Pearl, I have a question. This has been puzzling me for a very long time. I have heard the phrase "food for thought" many times. What is the best food for thought? Are there good foods for other things as well? Like, are there food groups for thoughts? Foods for good thoughts, or foods for bad ones? I am so hungry for your knowledge!

Pearl says:

Pearl of Knowledge shall feed you. First of all, there is only one basic food group: Cousin Pearlie Mae's Miracle Cure-All Squirrel Balls.

You don't need to know the ingredients because it is all advanced techno farming substrata micronutrient particle splitting and hydro mutations with variable soil constituency replacements. Suffice it to say, I've got it and you don't.

But you could become a distributor. Yes, really. Do you have lots of friends, Franny? Do you have parties in your nest box? Are you familiar with the term "pyramid"? Let ME know when you are ready and I will supply you with plenty of product, marketing strategies, a tummy sticker that reads, "Hungry? Ask Me," and a little tube of pink lipstick because that always comes with these things, don't ask ME why.

Remember, you offer health. You offer life. You, my friend Franny, can become a Pearl-a-marketer today! Kudos to you, kiddo. Welcome to the *force*.

–Pearl of Profiteering

Dear Pearl,

What exactly is channeling? How does it work?

S F

Pearl says:

Dear S F,

Channeling is when I, Pearl, superimpose myself upon a particular human's personality and thought processes.

I get to take over the brain and play and dance and do experiments. It's fun for ME. La la la la la la. I wish it was a better brain but I'm looking to expand. There's a jive-head Beat poet from the sixties who's available but I've got my eye on a rapper from Detroit with a vocabulary I can work with. Now do you understand?

Pearl of Illumination

Dear Pearl,

I think I'm in a midlife crisis. My dreams did not come true. I don't even want them anymore. I'm not proud of myself. And there is no one to witness my life. Does this sound like depression? Will a red sports car help? I tried drinking my troubles away, but it made me sick. Internet dating dejected me as I deplore being rude. How can I get out of this black hole before I succeed at suicide?

What should I do, Pearl?

Sincerely,

Archy

Pearl says:

I have two words for you, Archy: ping-pong.

....

Dear Pearl of Wisdom,

I live in your old neighborhood. In fact, I was raised in your old house by your old Pink Mama; me and a baby bruiser named Burl. Now we both live outside and poop on your shrine. Here's the thing. I want Burl squirrel to move to another neighborhood. I hate Burl. He was mean to the housing inspector and he's mean to me. Can I kill Burl and still be a good squirrel?

Yours truly,
Blithe Spirit

Pearl says:

Whoa there, lil' missy, One thing at a time. If Burl was mean to the housing inspector, you will *all* be moving to another neighborhood, real soon.

And yes, you *can* kill Burl and still be a good squirrel. But what makes you think you're a good squirrel? Pooping on the Shrine of PEARL does *not* a good squirrel make. You are a bad squirrel, Ms. Spirit, a very bad squirrel. Clean up your act, little girl. And clean up my shrine. *Touto de suito!*

Then send a big atonement gift through the PayPal account, which is available for this purpose. Once you have detonated your good faith, then Pearl of Wisdom will help you kill Burl. Muzzle nuzzle Big Pink Mama for ME.

Pearl of Wisdom absolves herself of any and all responsibility for whatever may go terribly, terribly wrong as a result of taking her advice. Thank you for writing in and have a nice day.

Dear Pearl of Wisdom,

My name is Burl. This may sound crazy, but I think someone is trying to kill me. I'm writing to you because I don't want to scare my squirrel friend, Blithe. She is delicate.

What should I do?
Burl

Pearl says:

Dear Burl,

Pearl of Wisdom suspects that your relationship is on shaky ground. I think you should tell your squirrel friend how you feel. Remember, there are three rules to a good relationship: loquacion, loquacion, loquacion. It would also be a good idea to gift Pearl with a love offering through the PayPal account available for this purpose. Do not tarry. Life is short. Especially yours. We have great love for you. We are complete.

Once more, Pearl of Wisdom absolves herself of any and all responsibility for whatever may go terribly, terribly wrong as a result of taking her advice. Thank you for writing.

Dear Pearl,

What do you think the esoteric difference is between *ashraganda* and the *veta* in reference to the supreme transcendence of *mahat*?

Pearl says:

Six of one, half a dozen of the other.

Blessings,
Pranayama Pearl

Dear Pearl,

Have you authored any books?

I just can't get enough of your writings. I hang on your every word. I am moved and transformed by your every thought.

MORE, MORE, MORE!

In hope and admiration,
Roscoe L.

Pearl says:

Dear Mr. L,

Funny you should mention that. Due to a phenomenon known as Schrödinger's squirrel, in requesting a book you have willed it into existence. And such a fine book it is. Kudos to you, Mr. Lellyveld, kudos. Next stop: Oprah's book club.

Pearl de Poesie,
Squirrel of Letters

Dear Pearl,

Why is poo smelly?
Ted

Pearl says:

Hello Ted,

Actually mine is not. You'd know that if you took time to stop and smell the squirrel poo. But ME thinks your olfactory concern may be more with the product of your own elimination.

Are you perhaps ridding yourself of rancid spiritual toxins even now? Well bully for you. Bully. Be gone rancid spiritual toxins, be gone, I say! And if they be not gone, you can purchase a wee atomizer of Pearl de Purity's Poo Away, found only where the finest accoutrements of crap are sold. Or, you might consider an exclusive diet of fruit, nuts, bark, and bugs. Thank you for writing in and always remember, Pearl loves you, albeit from afar.

Dear Pearl,

Okay so I'm very unclear as to what you actually *are*. Are you a human that thinks they're a squirrel and thought that pretending to be a psychic would be a funny joke (even though it's not)? I mean really what are you, because I just think you're completely insane.

O.

Pearl says:

How kind of you to write, dear O. We found it in good taste to censor your language. You are clearly in need of loving counsel but I fear there are too many barriers between you and Pearl de Wisdom to connect at this time. Be of good cheer. Pearl wishes you well.

Dear Pearl,

I am wondering: why you are a dead squirrel? What will my future look like. Will I be a ballerina?

Chelsy

Pearl says:

I am a dead squirrel for the same reason you will be a ballerina.
Because we have dreams, Chelsy, *dreams*.

Hey Pearl,

I'm so confused . . . . Is this all real? Or is it a joke? Not to make fun of you if it were to be real, would just like to know.

Hallie

Pearl says:

It's all of that.

"There are more things in heaven and earth, Hallie,
Than are dreamt of in your philosophy."

William Shakespeare, *Hamlet*, act 1 scene 5

Pearl of Appropriation

Dear Pearl,

I have always been the type of girl to have more (platonic) guy friends than girlfriends. Lately though, this has become a bit of a problem and I don't feel as if it is working the same way it used to. Really, I just want more girlfriends now, but don't know how to get them. I'm really shy. Please help me out.

Thanks,

Tootie

Pearl says:

Hi Tootie,

Making friends should work much the same way for both guys and gals. Decide which ones you wish to befriend. Then find out what interests them; a pretty sure bet is themselves, and then listen, listen, *listen*. Simple. Foolproof. Not that I've ever done this myself, but I'm friends with everyone who listens to ME.

Good luck, Ms. Popularity to Be.

Pearl of Popularity Comprehension

Dear Pearl,

I am concerned that your channeler, Georgette, is quite the lunatic. Could you please tell me what kind of medication she is taking ?

Sincerely,

Mr. Jim

P.S. I love squirrels

Pearl says:

Good morning, Mr. Jim.

Yes, yes, the Pearl agrees with you completely. Georgette (which isn't her name at all. She's Pink Mama) is quite the lunatic. I don't know what she's taking, but she often has trouble channeling ME authentically. Gets it all wrong. For example, I use *very* colorful language, the primary color being blue. But PM's channel filter won't allow it. I say Potato and she says Potato, I say #&#$! and she says Tomato, Potato, Potato, #&#$!, Tomato—let's call the whole thing off. I have my eye on this rapper in Detroit but he doesn't believe in ME, so it's a bear getting through. But thank you, thank you, thank you for noticing that PM may be a washout.

Pearl of Like Mind

Dear Pearl,

A squirrel bit my son at a resort in Colorado. That wasn't you or one of your relatives, was it?

Pearl says:

Was your son holding out a lunchable munchable? A good rule of thumb, if your son still has one, is Don't Feed the Squirrels! If there is not enough natural food around we'll move on. It's not a problem. We don't need your handouts and it just sets us up to get in a whole lot of trouble . . . like here.

If your son was a child at the time, the bite should have gone to you. Oh, if this was a ground squirrel nothing applies. You never know what motivates those little pissants.

Pearl the Purist

Dear Pearl:
Why?
Travis

Pearl says:

Because it is, and what must be must be and self-expression is glorious and helping others aligns the rhythm of the heartbeat with the rhythm of spheres and because it makes ME happy. Most of all, that! It makes ME happy.

Pearl the Pleased to Reply

Dear Pearl,

I have seen many squirrels rendering advice. From Foamy to Secret to your august self, a veritable spectrum of arboreal Rodentia offer wisdom and skittering motions. It must be in the genome somewhere.

However, I have noticed that some squirrels have a vocabulary that would make a sailor blush and would crash the hard drives over at Urban Dictionary. Tell me, when you want to say a dirty word (and indeed, what would be dirty to a squirrel?), what do you say instead?

Thank you, O Muncher of Celestial Acorns.

Pearl says:

Be it known that I say exactly what I want all the time. It's this $#@% channeler of mine who %$#%^ everything up by using $^%*& (*&* #@!@ AND $@%&*%^ in place of the actual pearls. This just makes ME so #@##$%^ *^& &%## that I could &#$^.

Ommmm, ommmm. But I don't. Because I meditate. Ommmm. Thank you for asking.

Mystic Pearl of Peace and Depth, Great Depth, and Peace

Dearest Pearl,

I am a little bit concerned right now for the sanity of two friends. They say they are meant for each other and deeply, deeply in love. One of them wants to run away with the other . . . to Uzbekistan. It's quite frightening, really.

Tell me the way to break these two up, because it's not working out in any way, shape, or form. They are constantly in contact 24/7 and talk in the most bizarre ways, which is starting to scare everyone. They come from two different worlds. And they sound like they are talking about getting close and personal more than anything else, which is frightening. This whole thing happened over the course of two days. Two very long days.

Please help me with my problems. Thank you.

Pearl says:

Best thing you can do for your friends is chip in for two one-way tickets to Uzbekistan!
You're never too young or too old to celebrate crazy love.

Dear Pearl,

Pearl, do you think you'll ever try to publish a book of your oh-so-wise insights?

Pearl says:
Hello???

Dear Pearl,

What is the key to a happy life? And what's the best way to cook raw peanuts?

Missy

Pearl says:

The key to a happy life is substituting pecans, walnuts, filberts, or almonds in any recipe calling for peanuts.

Chef Pearl

Dear Pearl,

I wonder if you're lucky to those that come across you.

Pearl says:

When coming across ME, you have to ask yourself one question: Do I feel lucky? Well, do ya, punk?

Dirty Pearly

Dear Pearl,

Is it true that Pink Mama used to be a porn star in the seventies?

Pearl says:

The name was my suggestion and I fear I have erred. So unlike ME. Here's how it works. The names George, Georgette, and Georgina Spelvin have been used by several porn stars, actors playing two roles in the same play, and many others who simply did not want their real name associated with a particular project. Therefore, when one sees the name Georgette Spelvin, it is assumed they understand this is a person who prefers to remain anonymous.

In the seventies, everybody knew this. Today they think Pink Mama was a porn star. Nope. Sorry. But I could talk dirty for you.

Porno Pearl

Dear Pearl of Infinite Wisdom,

The last five years have been hard on this biped, and I wish to turn things around. Any suggestions on how I could get my groove back? I'm all out of mojo and if it weren't for bad luck I wouldn't have no luck at all, and that ain't right! A girl's gotta be able to have a reason to lift her head high, after all! Please Pearl, help me get (at least some of) my strut back as I'm not ready for the boneyard just yet!

Your supplicant,

Lost her groove in NY

Pearl says:

Dear Sweet Strutless,

Do NOT turn things around. Do NOT attempt to get your groove or strut back. Let it all go. Breathe in, breath out. Now, look for the surprise in front of you.

Pearl of I'm so friggin' smart I could just bust!

The Eternal Pearl

Dear Pearl,

When I was young I believed the house I lived in was haunted. Was it a product of my overactive imagination or was it real?

—R. C.

Pearl says:

Define "haunt." Plenty of us are often slipping through the veil to have a bit of harmless fun at your expense. Haunting, however, requires commitment. Imagination . . . to image in. Sounds like you "saw" a ghost, my friend. Maybe somebody got stuck. S#!t happens.

That's always sad because the real fun is to come and go at will. I've taken to popping back for the Calvert County Fair in Maryland each year, and I'm always checking out the latest "squirrel-proof" bird feeders. That's just the funniest thing ever.

Why don't you revisit your childhood home and ask the current occupants if the ghosts are still there? Hahaha, heehee, that would be funny.

Pearl, more of a ghost than a poltergeist.

Hello ME pearl,

I am eleven years old and I think your videos are very cute and funny. I (like many other kids my age) want to be an artist when I grow up, but it is hard to make a good career out of it, so what do you think would make my art unique?

Lucy

Pearl says:

What *is* your art, Lucy? Do you paint? Draw? Sculpt? Do animation? Sing? Dance? Write novels or poems or lyrics? Perform? Design homes or clothing or jewelry? Walk the high-wire? Play the piano or banjo or accordion? Make Proper Possum Care videos? Decorate cakes? Yodel?

Once we know what your art is, Lucy, then we can make it unique. For a human, eleven years old is a fine age to figure out your gifts and ambitions. For a squirrel, we handle it at about four months.

Good luck, Lucy! Get back to ME.

Your pal,
Pearl

Dearest Mother Pearl,

I am suffering from hyperthyroid disorder—my thyroid acts in a way that is not pleasing to my mind nor my bowels. My "doctor" (I don't believe in modern medicine) tells me I need to be cut open and have it ripped from my flesh, but I don't believe her. Instead, I come to you, great Pearl, for your wisdom and advice. What path must I take? Hasten in your response, please, the thyroid is getting to be unbearable.

En omnia perotis,
S

Pearl says:

Dear Stella,

First, do not panic. What's the worst thing that could happen? Worst-case scenario is that you come visit ME for a few weeks while you figure out your next move. *So many options*, and I'm the best hostess ever. Lots of nut souffles and hickory daiquiris.

However, if you are not yet ready for your transition, you may just have to let Missy Doctor cut you open and rip that gland from your flesh. You have "doctor" in quotes. Does that mean she just plays one on TV? Then, no, don't let her do it.

My family always knew how to heal everything naturally, with Mother Nature. Then I had this terrible accident as a baby and would have died of fever if this big pink human hadn't scooped me up and raced me off to her own Missy Doctor, who cut off my leg. I loved my leg, but to leave it attached would have ruined everything.

At first, it was hard to learn to live with a missing part, but I did it. You can do it. If they give you a choice, have them remove your leg instead. I have a whole bunch of tips to share on how to get through that. But they probably won't.

Most of us, including ME, believe that if our mind is just strong enough or pure enough or laser focused enough, we can think our way well. But I couldn't do it, and I'm PEARL for Pearl's sake.

Of course all that was before I became a megalomaniac and took over the operation of the Universe. You are right to look to ME for salvation, but think beyond the one small *Gilmore Girls*-loving body you currently possess. Meanwhile, stay away from seafood, as they presumably have always extended you the same courtesy.

Keep processing, Stella. Pearl LOVES you.

Keep the faith.

Dear Pearl,

I'm afraid the Illuminati is going to take my opossum. I am worried that the government is working with the aliens because my opossum has been acting weird and I believe it is because he is sensing something. The Illuminati have been big with the teenagers of this generation, and I'm scared they will take my opossum because I know he knows something. How can I protect my opossum, so it can in turn protect me?

Fiona

Pearl says:

Your opossum is a member of the Illuminati. *Run*, Fiona, and don't look back.

Your pal,
Mailer Demon

Dear Pearl,

Is there any way that I and my friend can meet you, perhaps over video chat? I am very intrigued by you, and I want to see if you are real and not a deity.

Fran

Pearl says:

Hey Fran,

I, ME Pearl, am an ascended squirrel currently residing in a galaxy far, far away—so, whereas the idea of a video chat is kind of sweet and all, the true logistics would cause exploding brains all over the universe, and I don't think you want that.

Best be pleased with the contact we have. It's already well beyond mind-boggling, yes? Yes!

Time to revisit the last line of *Mrs. Skeffington*.

Whisker brush,
Pearl

Dear Pearl,

I am a student in college and I have reached a spiritual crossroad. Lately I have been questioning my identity: do I follow the path that I have started on, or do I forge a new path into uncharted and even dangerous territory? I await your guidance. Thank you, you provide me with hope.

Eliav

Pearl says:

Why do either when I can provide you with a ducky little cult right here? Have you not been paying attention? ME, here, now, it's so simple. You are already home, Eliav. Welcome. And "lightly" is exactly how you should be questioning your identity.

Pearl, purveyor of all spiritual wisdom and grace and other stuff.

Dear Pearl,

I just had a few questions for you. Do you find that Georgette does an adequate job speaking on your behalf? What made you choose her as your pet human? Also, do you have any idea of what the future holds for humankind as a whole? Thank you for your time, Pearl.

Taylor

Pearl says:

Good question, Taylor! Georgette is an imbecile! I sent out a call and she was the only one who heard it. There must be a channel into the human world for ME, so being a pragmatist, I took what was there. Am always on the lookout for a better one.

The future of humankind depends entirely on respecting your mother. Gaia. Those who do must prevail over those who don't.

Watch the wildlife. We understand.

Pearl, who appreciates getting straight to the point along with a nice plate of spaghetti now and again.

Dearest Pearl de Wisdom,

We are going off to college soon and we don't know what direction our lives should be going in. Could you offer any sage squirrel advice on how to move on to bigger and better things?

Much love,
Skippy and Pip

Pearl says:

West.

Definitely west!

You're welcome.

The P

Dear Pearl,

Do you know about the great Tim Tooten?
B.

Pearl says:

Yup.

Do you know about the great Nellie Bly?
P.

Hi Pearl,

I think the squirrels in my lawn are plotting to take my house over. When I pull in my driveway, they will be congregated around the tree closest to my lawn, but when they see me they all disperse. I think it's because they don't want me to hear their plans? Please help, Pearl. I am very concerned.

Jim

Pearl says:

Hey Jim,

If your suspicions are correct, you might just as well move out now and find another place to live. Unless, of course, you can share with wildlife, but so few humans are able to do that. Save yourself a lot of grief and just give it to them. Although why they would prefer your house over a genuine, grow-out-of-the-ground tree is a mystery.

People, if you are having trouble with squirrels, I am not your best source of succor. Think about it.

Even so, Pearl loves you. All of you (with only a few exceptions, and you can guess who you are).

Dear Pearl,

I have just been blessed with raising a baby opossum (that will eventually be an educational outreach possum) that has lost one of its eyes. I feel like she now has trust issues because of this. Do you have any advice for making my opossum trust me? Also, we originally thought baby possum was a boy, but now we think it's girl. We've already named it Bruce. Any questions about how we should approach Bruce on the issue of telling him "he" is actually a "she"? I am a firm believer of the fluidity of gender identity, but I'd like advice on how to approach the subject with the utmost sensitivity.

Your most devoted follower,
Mimo

Pearl says:

Congratulations, Mimo. You are, indeed, blessed to have an opossum. You will gain her trust by engaging exclusively in trustworthy behaviors. You are funny to presume that Bruce needs you to explain her gender. The hubris of humans never ceases to astonish.

This is a rare gift, Mimo. Observe her and serve her, and you will grow wise.

Dear Pearl,

My opossum has been threatening to take out life insurance on me for the past several months and I'm starting to grow worried about the intent. Is this a bluff or should I be concerned?

Pearl says:

Threatening for several months and you're just now starting to worry? Psychic Pearl sees a Darwin Award in your future.

DUCK!

Just kidding!

P

Dear Pearl,

I'm curious: how does one domesticate a possum?

Curious

Pearl says:

Hi Curious,

You don't domesticate a possum. Possums will domesticate themselves if and when they feel like it.

Dear Pearl,

I've been having trouble with my health lately, and am seeking new all-natural remedies. Are there any potions or creations you can suggest that will boost both my mental and physical powers? I come to you humbly, understanding that your wisdom is great and your spirit is strong.

Chester the Blowfish

Pearl says:

It must be exhausting being a blowfish. Both your problem and solution have to do with breath. Breathe easy, Chester. Breathe slower, deeper, fuller.

Meditate by getting very still and counting your exhalations and the rest of the answer will come to you. I'm also picking up a mineral imbalance. Triple your vegetable intake and *breathe*. Pull power from the center of the earth.

Pearl loves you.

Hi Georgette,

You are a beautiful and sincere woman and if you're single, I would love to talk with you. I fell down the YouTube rabbit hole and there you were. I was instantly smitten. You have my email, I'm looking forward to hearing from you.

Michael

Pearl says:

I might be willing to pimp out my human for the right price.

Numbers, Michael, numbers.
Pearl, Procurer to the Stars, literally

Dearest Pearl of Infinite Knowledge,

A mysterious Christmas present has appeared in our dorm. We do not know which of us it is for, who it is from, or what is in it. Can you, oh mighty and all-knowing Pearl, answer for us any of these questions? Thank you for your squirrely knowledge.

Love,
Buddie

Pearl says:

Take a giant pair of tongs and drop it in the nearest body of water. Don't look back.

Dearest Pearl,

I have an opossum-killing tendency. My dad raised me to hate opossums and kill them any chance I get. I have killed two opossums with my car and can't seem to stop my instincts from killing opossums. Any suggestions?

Cal

Pearl says:

Hi Cal,

The fact that you are writing fills ME with hope and happiness. You may not even know you are serious about changing, but Pearl knows and Pearl celebrates you. Possums are great for the environment and do no harm to anyone. Golden rule, Cal, golden rule.

....

Pearl,

I was walking my dog yesterday and something very strange happened. I heard a voice calling to me from the nearby trees. It went: "Hello . . . *hello*." I looked and the only thing I could see was a squirrel. Do you think it was in trouble? This is not the first time a squirrel has talked to me before. I think I have a spiritual connection to squirrels. Please offer me some guidance in this trying time.

xoxo,
Jimbo

Pearl says:

Hey Jimbo!

So happy to welcome you into the family. When we're in trouble we bark and chatter and leave no doubt. What you describe sounds more like a pleasant psychic connection. But now that you are "on the radar," stay alert. You will likely be called into service. You have been chosen, Jimbo. It's an honor and a responsibility and you are worthy. Praise ME.

Pearl

Dear Pearl,

Today, my best friend died. My dear squirrel, Apollo Hammy Jr. (Hams for short) passed on when my neighbors stupidly left some rat poison out. So I was devastated, and I want to make sure Hams got a good send-off. Are there, like, any squirrel burial rituals that you would recommend? How would you want to say goodbye to your best friend, Pearl?

Belle

Pearl says:

So sorry for your loss, Belle.

We squirrels have a spiritual life other than what humans imagine. When I passed over, my human buried me in a little white prayer scarf like a Buddhist monk. It was *so silly*, but I loved her for loving ME and wanting to honor ME somehow.

In truth, Hams is with ME now experiencing a joyous freedom unlike any other. What is left for you is to celebrate the relationship that has passed. Gather those items that remind you of Hams. Write down what was special about your relationship and how it improved your life. Flowers and candles tend to feel good at these times. Invite a trusted friend to witness the ritual. This is effective with or without the body being present.

The closure is for you, Belle, and it's important that you have it. I'm sure that the spirit of Hams will show up to support you and if you are very still you will feel sweet warm squirrel breath on your neck. Otherwise Hams is doing just fine. Trust ME on this.

Dear Pearl,

I soon confirmed my darkest suspicions. The squirrels, it appeared, often lived in trees. Now I knew the true reason behind the "tree-hugging" liberal-pinko environmental movement. It wasn't to save the world. It was to protect the squirrels.

Pearl says:
Same thing.

Dear Pearl,

Is time travel something we on this plane should pursue?
Say, for whatever reason, that your apartment is strewn with a dozen old microwave ovens, several industrial magnets and miles of power transmission-grade copper cable that you found by the beach. Should someone in possession of these items build a time machine?

Asking for a friend.

Pearl says:

Sure, Asking, tell your friend to keep building his time machine. The secret ingredient: a liberal sprinkling of lug nuts.

You, however, shouldn't bother, because time travel needn't be labor intensive. Possums used to do it all the time, but gave it up after discovering that nothing has changed in seventy million years. It's all a matter of perspective and spaghetti. Never underestimate the power of spaghetti. It will take you wherever you want to go. But remember: you've probably already been there.

Your pal,
Prescient Pearl

Dear Pearl,

I think you are on some awesome drugs. I love opossums too. I would be very interested in learning what you are on . . . .

Pearl says:

Squirrels don't do drugs because, well, think about it . . . squirrels on methamphetamines would be redundant.

Your pal,
Pearl

Dear Pearl,

I am very inspired by your work and I hope to one day be as enlightened as you are. Any suggestions to reach the knowledge that I seek? Thank you, much love.

Pearl says:

Excellent question! Sadly you never will be as enlightened as ME. There can only be one ME Pearl. But be glad. This much enlightenment can be a crushing responsibility. Remember, "To whom much is given much will be" however that phrase goes. To continue evolving at the fastest rate possible, study nature. She will show you everything you need to know to best *be* in the world.

Pay particularly close attention to squirrels. All creatures are created equal, except for squirrels. We're better. It's a simple fact. Let s/he who has tufted pointy little ears hear.

Hello, Lord of Everything Holy.

My one question to you on this fine summer's morn is one of great virtue. What should I eat for dinner?

Thank you ever so,
Fillipe

Pearl says:

First off, Fillipe, I am *Lady* of All Things Holy and Otherwise.

For dinner you should have spaghetti and Queen Anne cherries. This is always the default dinner so you need never be in this quandary again. In a pinch, red cherries will do but strive for Queen Annes.

You're welcome.

Hi MEpearl,

What are we to do with our lives? Are we not destined to die, so why try anyways? Is our path through these woods preordained or can we truly control our direction? What is the meaning of it all?

Ralph

Pearl says:

I'm glad you asked, Ralph.

1. Be kind to squirrels.

2. Be kind to every other living creature, especially yourself.

3. Forget about being "well rounded." Focus on your gifts, those things you do really well, and do those.

4. Be kind to squirrels.

Do these things and you will fall in love with life and with yourself and that's what it's all about. Destined to die? Well yes and no. Think of a squirrel doing somersaults; rolling under, die, rolling up, reborn, over and over and over. Take ME for example. I've incarnated numerous times until I found perfection as a squirrel and made my final ascension. But I'm kind of a bodhisattva, both ascended and remaining behind to give my beloveds the occasional push and keep them merrily rolling along. It's all perfect except for one major glitch: the food chain. But be assured I am working on a system where no one has to kill to eat. Hope this gives you something to gnaw on.

Pearl loves you~

I have so much to tell you.

Dear Pearl,

My opossum is going out on her first date with a friend's opossum and is nervous about accessorizing. How can we bring out her golden brown eyes and sparkling personality? Thanks for your time. Jeffrina Kelby (my baby girl) thanks you too.

Pearl says:

Hello!

While we would love to help you accessorize for a first date, something in your post takes precedence. If Jeffrina Kelby has golden brown eyes, she's not an opossum. You now have a lot to think about, so I'll leave you to it.

Pearl, the all-pervasive Voice of Everything

Dear Pearl,

I am a college freshman and wanted some tips for a successful year. Thanks!

Pearl says:

You have come to the right source for inspiration and wisdom. Although I am, personally, an autodidact, I appreciate higher education with all of my little jackhammer heart.

Most college campuses have squirrels and most well-meaning students feed them junk. Don't let this be you. Tip one: shelled walnuts. Feed gingerly because your thumb resembles a walnut and you can't blame them for a mishap.

Also, your brain resembles a walnut encased in your skull shell. Think about it. Ancient warriors used to eat the brains of respected fallen foes in order to become smarter. You are bound to run into very smart professors at college. You can either spend years studying with these scholars or you can simply eat their brains. The choice is yours. Thank you for coming to ME with your concerns. I trust you've not been disappointed.

Your mentor,

Pearl

Most Honorably Revered MEPearl,

Your large pink human channel embodies such a unique combination of beauty, coyness, and yet grace that it leaves me stupefied with attraction and unable to fully absorb your transcendent wisdom. I must confess I have even allowed myself to believe at times that the wisdom may come from her rather than you. What, besides a cold shower, might help me overcome this distraction?

Pearl says:

Big Pink is a disappointing human. Even so, she's MINE. And you don't want to mess with an ascended squirrel!

Hi,

I was wondering how I should help a squirrel that came to me and I saw that it was injured in its leg. I don't know how to care for it well. Please help.

Thanks!

Pearl says:

Lovely question. Rule of thumb: If you can't catch it, it can probably get by on its own.

If you do catch it and there is an injury, don't hesitate to go to a veterinarian or wildlife center.

We squirrels are complex creatures, physically and psychologically. We require highly specialized care. Please leave the helping to those who know how. However, for being such a mensch, Pearl has just expunged your most embarrassing memory from your permanent record. You're welcome.

Dear Pearl,

My friends and I are terrified by the clown attacks rising in our area. What can we do? Is this a punishment?

Pearl says:

Dear FBC (Frightened by Clowns),

Even at the best of times, clowns are no laughing matter. But clowns gone bad are a bane forever. To even question if this is a punishment suggests that, at some time in your life, you have been guilty of clown abuse. Have you and your friends ever bullied a clown? Perhaps a baby clown who has grown up and is out to settle a score.

To express remorse and solidarity you might start wearing vastly oversized shoes and a fright wig. Perhaps you and all of your friends could ride about town jammed into a MINI Cooper. You might jump out at people and beat them about the head and neck with a rubber chicken or squirt seltzer down their pants. If you follow these instructions you will begin to see clown attacks in a whole new light, almost like a sporting event. *Become what you fear.* Thank you for writing in and have a nice day.

Dear Pearl,

I bring good news!

Over two years ago I asked you for advice. I used to get ignored any time I would open my mouth. It seemed like nobody could hear me, or no one cared enough to listen. But you came to me during my time of need, telling me to get quieter and embrace pith. *And it worked*. I'm a much quieter person now, but any time I speak people really listen to me. I actually feel important, almost like a different person. It's incredible, I've grown so much in such a short amount of time and it's all thanks to you. I really appreciate it, Pearl, you truly are wise. I pray that one day I may become as wise as you and spread your knowledge to the masses, to help all those in need.
Much love <3

Cristine

Pearl says:

Good news, indeed, Cristine! You delight ME. If only more of your kind would *embrace pith*!

Now, you will never become as wise as ME, so let that go and pick up some spaghetti. Yes, spaghetti. Many do not realize the immense healing properties of spaghetti. You can eat it, play with it, and best of all, make art with it.

Now that you are important, you are ready for spaghetti art. Trust me. Go deep and bring your secrets into the light. Go wild. Send images. Pearl loves you.

Dear Pearl,

I have liked this guy for two years and I wish he would like me back. During this school year, he seemed to act interested in me, staring at me and he just seemed to light up when he would talk to me. I was too shy to talk to him then, and I guess he thought I was uninterested. He stopped staring at me and that glow went away, and he has a girlfriend now. Is it ever too late to try to get him to like me again?

Lynne

Pearl says:

Dear Lynne,

What a wonderful learning experience for the next human who becomes smitten with you. When you recognize "that look," acknowledge it, but *only* if you're smitten in return. Do not mess with someone else's relationship. There are many more nuts in the tree and they'll fall at your feet with just a little shaking. If shy is who you are then be shy until you are comfortable being otherwise.

Trust that you are lovable. Pearl knows. Pearl loves you.

Hi Pearl,

I'm not sure if things will work out for me and my boyfriend. He's mean to me and we have different political views. He also doesn't like opossums. What should I do?

Pearl says:

Things already have *not* worked out for you with this boyfriend. If he's mean to you he must go. Immediately. I could send the Squirrel Liberation Army after him but that would be costly and he could die. Move out, move away, move on.

Personally, I don't care for possums either. Funny the cards I deal out, even to myself. Take care of yourself and the animals you love. This fellow will only hold you back and down. Expel him from your heart. Become the sovereign queen of your own life.

Dear Pearl,

I have been trying to conceive for ten years. I am twenty-eight years old. Will it ever happen?

Pearl says:

Well, that depends . . . .What, exactly, are you trying to conceive and what, exactly, have you been doing for the past ten years to conceive it? The devil's in the details, dearie. When you're ready let ME know.

Your Pearl

Hello Pearl,

My friends and I would like to know if it is possible for humans and other animals to be connected on the same astral plane that squirrels and opossums can be?

Pearl says:

What?

Dear Pearl,

I crashed my P-51 Mustang before I could ask for insurance. It got shot down by German squirrels, though I'm happy to be alive because I managed to eject. Do you have any tips on my next step on life?

Sean

Pearl says:

I find it odd that you seek out a squirrel for guidance on your next step, when it was a squirrel who caused your calamity.

BTW, there are no German squirrels. We have no allegiance to artificial boundaries, except those made by pee.

I sense you are an impetuous fellow, Sean. Your next step is mastery over self, self-discipline, delayed gratification. If you can achieve this quality the rest of your life will be golden.

You're welcome in advance.

Prophet Pearl

Dear Pearl,

I hope you're having a lovely summer. I would like to know, how is it possumble for you to have so many great gifts, like your talent, your possums, and the gift of *love*. Where can I find *love*? I lost my *love* somewhere and now I feel empty as a hollowed-out tree. You are my last hope.

Feelings of gratitude,
Lizzie

Pearl says:

Dear Lizzie,

You have many, many, many hopes beyond ME. But next time you lose *love*, come to ME first not last. If you have feelings of gratitude you have not lost your *love*, only misplaced it. Even I, the great and powerful Pearl, sometimes feel empty as a hollowed-out tree. It's true! You are not alone, far from it. First, express these feelings to your animal friends (then make some!) whom you know won't judge you. Then ask some of your favorite humans if they have ever felt as you do. Profound bonding will ensue. Do this at least three times and your *love* will reappear bigger and brighter and better than ever. Either that or the bunch of you will just barrel over a cliff together. It could go either way.
At least, Pearl loves you~

Hello Pearl!

I'm a big fan and opossum lover! I was considering owning an opossum as a pet but I've gotten so many mixed responses like, they're expensive and very prone to bone diseases but they're cuddly and loving and fun to have. Your big pink human caretaker seems to have owned and taken care of many lovely, beautiful opossums. Is it worth it, and what are some very important key things to know before jumping into being an opossum owner? I'm very curious and would love to get some advice from an expert. Lots of love to you and all your lovely pets!

Pearl says:

Don't do it! It's a terrible idea. The worst. Forget about it. It will only lead to heartbreak. Think puppies or kittens or a house bunny.

As a dead squirrel and Goddess of the Universe, I must protest the use of the word "own" in regard to wildlife, or any animal. As for caregiving, sharing space, time and resources, and bonding, that's different. In that case, when it comes to possums, NO! Don't get one. Big Mistake. You'd regret it. NO! And because I am ME, Pearl the omniscient, I know that you won't heed a word of this. You are too far in. But, at least, get some hands-on training first. Volunteer to assist local rehabilitators or to intern at a wildlife center. Foster first. Learn firsthand why you've been warned.

Your pal,

Pearl

....

Hello again Pearl!

Thank you so much for responding to my question! I would like to follow up on what you said. I did mean caregiving and bonding and such. I love opossums so much and would like to experience taking care of one. I will heed your advice and volunteer or intern (whichever comes first) at a wildlife center and try to get the best hands-on experience possible. (P.S. I would greatly appreciate your thoughts on cats and rats; I love cats a bunch and someone very close to me loves rats. What do you think about these two animals?)

Pearl says:

Good show!

Rats live three years, cats can live twenty years. What kind of commitment are you up for? "You become responsible forever for what you've tamed." (*The Little Prince*)

Dear Pearl,

Does Pink Mama have a day job? Or does she do this for a living?

Pearl says:

What Pink Mama does when she is not entirely devoted to ME is of little consequence.

Dear Pearl,

I am afraid of being alone. Who shall I date, male, female? Any hints on where to look?

Pearl says:

Go to the first town to the west of you large enough to have a rec center attached to the park. Find the ping-pong area, grab a paddle, and the first creature that asks you to play is your soul mate. You're welcome.

Most Precious Pearl,

Do you think I'll ever find the fortune and praise that I hunger for so much in this short but quick life that I'm living? Very sorry if this is a vain and selfish question, but everyone wonders this at least once in their life.

Jesus

Pearl says:

Dear Jesus,

I doubt that anyone has ever done better in either regard.

Your pal,
Pearl

Dear you, Pearl,

I just started going back to school after a long while, and I am overwhelmed by the amount of work and stress it is causing me. My question is, do you have any study tips or coping tips, and do you believe I can do it?!

Lots of love,
Sophie

Pearl says:

Dear Sophie: I'm not the Rah! Rah! You can do it! type of squirrel. Of course you *can* do it, but that is not the issue. Stress is the issue and figuring out how to reduce it to a manageable size. Something must be eliminated or postponed. Yes, *that*! You know exactly what can go or wait. Do yourself a favor and downsize. This may mean putting your kids up for adoption. No one will criticize you for making a brave decision.

Your pal Pearl

Dear Pearl,

Can I book you to perform a speech at my best friend's wedding in June?

Pearl says:

Yes, but it would be a mistake since I see little hope for couples starting out these days.

P

Dear Pearl,

Oh, bushy-tailed Seer of all, please allow me to be enlightened with your boundless knowledge. The woman I love is hesitant to open up to me completely about her thoughts and feelings for fear of me being like her former suitors who would ridicule and torment her because of her thoughts. I humbly ask that you would advise her about what she should do.

Tiger

Pearl says:

Dear Tiger,

She doesn't need my advice, you do. Stay out of her personal thoughts and feelings. She'll tell what she wants you to know when she wants you to know it. Respect her boundaries. Back off and lighten up.

Your pal,

Pearl

Dear Pearl,

I have seen that many people have asked you questions about how to live a more enjoyable life and you have given great answers. I have a question about how to tell someone I admire deeply how much I care about them. I would like to create a greater connection with them but I am scared to show my feelings. Thank you.

With greatest regards,

Tory

Pearl says:

Tory,

Don't tell them anything. Really. Don't. Show them. Either: Ask for their help on a sincere issue where they would be a logical source of help, then let them help you. Not easy but very bonding. Or offer them help which they appear to need and you are qualified to offer. In both cases sincerity is essential. If you can't be absolutely sincere then don't do it.

Your pal,

Pearl

Dear Pearl, dead squirrel.

Buddha has failed me. I know what I want to do in life but I don't want to go and do it. May your words guide me outside this grey paradox.

Pearl says:

Maybe you failed Buddha.

Dear Pearl,

You have changed my life and since I believe in you so much I am sure you can force my future since you are a true squirrel god. Can you give me a small prophesy of my future? Like will I travel the world? Who will I marry? Will I be successful? What does life have in store for me? I believe in you and I believe that you will have some prophesy for me.

Pearl says:

Well, no, not really. At least not anything that I'm going to tell you. The questions you have are intended to be answered in the moment through experience. Being told the likeliest scenarios of your future would be more of a hindrance than a help. You'd just get in the way and then fate would have to make an example of you. Just take the next indicated action and, above all, be kind. Your future should unfold brilliantly. Be careful about asking for "spoiler alerts." They are called that for a reason.
Pearl loves you.

Hello Pearl,

What is Cinanomon?

Pearl says:

It's the properation of two thracknels and a grall.

You're welcome.

Dear Pearl,

I've done my taxonomic research and found what I regard to be the best rodent. Though some call them squirrels, anomalures are not closely related to sciurids. The body of an anomalure is far more robust and sexier. Some even have skin flaps for gliding. How do you feel not being the best rodent?

Clayton

Pearl says:

Silly Clayton.

Pearl loves you.

Dear Pearl,

I've been having a bit of trouble dealing with long-term stress, and I don't wish for it to affect my mood and disposition as it seems to have already.

I know a goddess [such] as yourself experiences naught such troubles, but if you were to, how would you deal?

Pearl says:

You don't think being Goddess of the Multiverse is stressful? Thank ME for funny cat videos.

Dear Pearl,

What do you think of Baby Yoda?

Pearl says:

I don't.

O mighty Pearl, I seek your wisdom.

How do I get rid of the rats' nest currently situated in my car? They are not very friendly and I am too scared to tempt their tempers another time.

Yours,
Greg

Pearl says:

Dear Greg,

Squatters rights. Time to get a new car.

With love,
Pearl

Hello Pearl,

Over the past few weeks I have been living rough on Skid Row in Los Angeles, CA, and many of the tent-dwelling mongrels who are unfortunately my "neighbors" keep taking my belongings! These include two needles completely unrelated to drugs or any illegal activity, and two pill bottles of Viagra I use as a supplement and definitely not for sexual activities. Can you give me advice as to how I can make more friends in my homeless encampment to avoid my belongings being taken?

Much thanks,

Jason

Pearl says:

So, your question is, "How can I make more friends?"

Answer: Kindness.

Dear Pearl,

How do you make milk for a baby goat?

Pearl says:

OK, I give up. How do you make milk for a baby goat?

Hey Pearl!

I have a problem . . . the Illuminati are coming after me. I can't trust anyone or anything. What should I do? Please help I'm going to die.

Pearl says:

Sage advice: If you can't beat 'em, join 'em. It's fun being part of the Illuminati. There are costumes and you can play with really cool eccentrics. So stop running and welcome what chases you. Very empowering. And, no, you are not going to die. Not from this, anyway. But do be careful climbing trees that grow at a precarious angle.

Your pal,

Pearl

Hey Pearl,

I am a concerned dog.

Writing about my addiction for chasing scared little squishy squirrels. How do I conquer my inner dog? I've tried tea, and yoga, mostly doing downward dog. If squirrels are the universe, am I a black hole? I feel empty. Help me, sacred squishy universal goddess.

ImaDog

Pearl says:

What's the matter with you, ImaDog??? Don't you have any toys of your own? You are engaged in the most egregious of behaviors with far-reaching consequences. Regular karma is a dance in the park compared to *sacred squirrel* karma.

We come after your puppies, and your puppies' puppies, and your puppies' puppies' puppies, and their humans.

Next time you feel drawn to the chase, just say no. Too hard? Then redirect your attention. I recommend birds.

Chasing birds is huge fun and in the unlikely event that you catch one, you will be celebrated, not shunned, as is the case with small-minded, mean-spirited, inbred, caca for brains intent on savaging my multitudinous beloveds.

Each squirrel released into your planet is a genuine part of the great and powerful ME and what you do to the least of my squirrelettes, you also do unto ME. So don't! Because if you do, with ME as my witness, you'll regret the day you were ever whelped.

P.S. You should not know we are squishy.

Love,
Pearl

⋯⋯

Dear Pearl,

I wanted to know what your opinion on the use of medical marijuana was, and if you think it is beneficial to the future of medicine.

Joe B.

Pearl says:

Whatever gets you through the night, Joe.

⋯⋯

Dear Pearl,

My coworkers are not convinced of your excellence. What advice do you have to win them over with you and your opossum?

Love,
Olive

Pearl says:

Dear Olive,

I have you and that is what matters. My followers need not Pearlselytize. Everyone comes to ME in my own good time.

Pearl the Patient

Dear Pearl,

Oh great and mighty Pearl, if you had the ability to die again, would you prefer to be gored by a bull or eaten by a ravenous dog?
I seek your wisdom.

Pearl says:

You are right to seek my wisdom if those are the only options you can offer. You would do well to read more, particularly the classics. As a squirrel I had to eat the classics, which can make one irregular, if you catch my drift. This is one of the few instances where you are lucky to be human. Start with *Wuthering Heights* and *Gypsy*, then ask ME what you really want to know.
Pearl loves you.

Dear Pearl,

I'm feeling frustrated with having to "try" around people. It's exhausting.

I just want to show up and be myself with no pretenses, but I don't know if people really know what to do with that.

Women are expected to be polite, accommodating, give compliments, be bubbly, etc., and sometimes I'm feeling very internal and quiet.

I get tired just thinking about all the social conduct puzzles and would rather be more in the background, making things for people to enjoy.

I'm wondering if you have any advice . . . . Should I come to terms with needing to try hard at times or acclimate to holding the tension when I don't feel like adhering to social standards? Thanks in advance.

Julia

Pearl says:

Oh Julia, Julia, Julia.

You are *really* angry. Own it and express it, preferably while hurling fistfuls of spaghetti any ol' where. Your condition calls for *lots* of spaghetti. Don't stint. Also, as a squirrel, my go-to move is to bite my adversaries really hard. Guaranteed to get their attention. Try it. You'll like it.

Your P

Dear Pearl,

I am utterly useless when it comes to romance and in desperate need of guidance. I've been seeing a man that I think I like but every date leaves me with conflicted feelings. How do I make sense of my own heart?

Blessings to you and yours,
Edna

Pearl says:

Listen up, Edna!

Your heart makes perfect sense. It knows you are not with the right person. Once you are, you will not be conflicted. You will be simply and happily insane.

Pearl the Profound

Hello Pearl!

I'm a young girl who met a boy a long time ago. He and I started dating and were very happy together. However, not long into the relationship, he broke up with me over the phone. We were not perfect. I have done him wrong and he has damaged me as well. My greatest problem is that I cannot stop feeling those same romantic feelings I had for him so long ago. I would like to quit but my heart still flutters around him. Oh, majestic Pearl, please give me advice on how to get over him! Thank you for reading, it is greatly appreciated.

Pearl says:

Early loves never lets go. Get used to it. One day you will hear that he has died and feel relieved. Or is that just ME?

Dear Pearl,

I am infatuated with someone who is currently unavailable, yet I know they have interest in me as well. I know I must nurture the relationship further before anything else happens, but I am just longing for something more. I cherish this person and ultimately just want to be close to them. My heart is just wrapped up in this fantasy that I know has a great possibility of becoming reality—but does it? Sometimes I feel like I get carried away by all the different possibilities but I know what my heart wants!

Thank you dearest Pearl. I appreciate your time and energy. You are beloved.

Pearl says:

Yes, the heart wants what the heart wants, but if getting it will lead to chaos and suffering it may be best to just say no. Your heart will want again, they always do.

Pearl loves you.

Dearest all-knowing Pearl,

Do you think it is ethical for teenagers to twerk and grind on each other at school?

Sincerely,
A traumatized teacher.

Pearl says:

I do not consider the described behavior to be an ethical matter. It surprises ME that a teacher would use that term in this context.

I ain't called Pearl de Wisdom for nothin', kiddo. As to the appropriateness of the behavior, that would depend on what kind of school it is and what the students came to learn.

Pearl de Wisdom

Dear Pearl,

I got into a relationship with a guy a few months ago, even when we both knew that we didn't have much time left together. Now we live three thousand miles apart and we know it will be almost impossible to ever meet again, but we still talk everyday even knowing it won't work out. What should I do?

Thanks in advance.

Pearl says:

Change your attitude ASAP.

You're welcome.
P

Dearest Divine Pearl Messiah,

I need your help!! I have no motivation to do anything in my life. What can I do? What do you do? Help me, please!

Yours devoted,
Joseph

Pearl says:

Always ask yourself, *What would Pearl do in this situation?* but never actually do that. It only works for ME. Seems you were motivated to contact ME so perhaps a career in communications awaits. Don't worry about what should motivate you; only pay attention to what *does* motivate you. Therein lies your energy, your happiness, your purpose. Also, are you getting enough spaghetti? Never underestimate the power of refined carbohydrates.
Pearl loves you!

Pearl

How do I break out of the capitalist machine?

Kraydor

Pearl says:

I've given this a great deal of thought and I just don't care. Even so, Pearl loves you, Kraydor.

Oh great and powerful MEPearl,

I wish to please you. I wish to dedicate my life to you as one dedicates their life to a deity. I wish to be the source of your greatest happiness. I wish to write songs about you. I wish to paint you. Though I know no form of art may even remotely capture your greatness. How can I please you, oh MEPearl? From this point on, my body exists to be your instrument of servitude!

Pearl says:

Of course, you do and Bully! But let's look at a few specifics.

"I wish to dedicate my life to you as one dedicates their life to a deity." This is redundant.

"I wish to be the source of your greatest happiness." Well, dear, only I can be that, don't you know.

"How can I please you, oh MEPearl?" Use sending $ as the default. People tend to get peevish on that point but when one is bold enough to ask the question Pearl can be no less than omnihonest.

Yes, yes, I do inspire art and literature and music and why not choreograph me a ballet at some point? You certainly have the right idea. Double Bully! Bully! Bully! Your body offering is swell but I'll require your psyche as well, capisce? In for a penny, in for a pound, tra la tra la. Welcome dedicant. And if you ever need anything, anything at all, just work it out.

Your everything,
ME

Dear Pearl,

I have fallen in love with a man whose parents do not want us to be together because we do not have the same beliefs and we are not the same ethnicity. I have tried to reach out to them, but they fake illness so that they won't speak to me, or to make their son feel guilty. We are grown adults and should be able to make our own decisions, yet they hold us hostage by their prejudices and ignorance. I am so desperate for a solution or any idea on how to solve this.

Sincerely Yours.

Pearl says:

Dear Sincerely Yours,

You have written your own solution. You say, "We are grown adults and should be able to make our own decisions." Well, you *are* able to make your own decisions and it seems that you are deciding to be held hostage by his parents' prejudices. *Make another decision.* His parents are not responsible for your happiness, *you* are. If he loves you back then be together. His parents will come around or they won't. All you can do is stay loving and keep the welcome mat out and dusted. If, however, the gentlemale in question is choosing his parents over you (and there may be good reason for this), then move on, my friend. So much love and life awaits you. Never stay stuck, says Pearl.

Hello there, Pearl,

I am wondering what you would do in my shoes. I am not sure whether to go down the road less traveled or the road that's easier.

Thanks xoxo,
Wanderlust

Pearl says:

Greetings, Wanderlust.

You are wise in understanding that much depends on your shoes. Open-toed stilettos or flip-flops definitely beg the road that's easier. Let ME know where you wander on your road to ME. All roads lead to Pearl, eventually.

Dear Pearl,

I think you are wonderful and you make me laugh. My question is, my mama and my gramma both got cancer this year and it's been very hard [as] both are doing chemo. Pearl, will things ever be OK again? Will I ever be as happy as I was? I just seem to be very angry at how things are, but I don't know if I'll ever be the same again. Anyway, thanks for your time.

Sooni

Pearl says:

Sweet Sooni,

You will never be the same again. You will find a new happiness that comes from knowing your mother and grandmother better than ever before. And their relationship will mend in places they didn't even know were broken. And it will never be the same.

There is cancer in my family too. Yes, squirrels get cancer. Research shows that Cleopatra had Graves' disease, which has nothing to do with you but I thought I'd mention it.

Couragio! (That's Italian. I learned it from a Canadian.)

Your pal,
Pearl

Dear Pearl,

What should I name my son?

Pearl says:

Radish.

Dear Pearl,

How can I believe that you really have such wisdom?

Pearl says:

Easiest thing, there isn't much to it.

All you gotta do is doodily do it.

Words to Ponder by Pearl

Nope. Just ME, Pearl.

About Pearl and Georgette

Pearl de Sagesse de Sabaduria de Wisdom de Tout, also known as Pearl de Wisdom or ME Pearl, is an all-knowing, all-powerful squirrel deity and an internet sensation. Pearl lived for twelve years in Southern California under the care of Georgette Spelvin, known to Pearl as Pink Mama, an oddly sentimental witchy woman and licensed wildlife rehabilitator. In captivity, Pearl gained omniscience by gnawing her way through most of the Merriam-Webster English dictionary and bits of the Larousse Spanish and French and by using her seven senses to absorb vast amounts of information (the rest she makes up). The very model of a modern psychic squirrel, Pearl ascended to the heights of psychic prowess, surpassing all other animals, people, and plants. After her death, Pearl's mission became to aggrandize herself through religion, politics, social media, cult formation, charitable contributions, and syndicated advice columns, as the divine Pearl fully expects anyone who comes in contact with her to benefit beyond their wildest dreams. Using Georgette as her mouthpiece and conduit, she continues her work as a prophet online by providing sage life advice for the masses on her website, MEPearl.com, and through the YouTube channel, MEpearlA, where she has more than 124,000 subscribers and shares videos relating to the proper care and keeping of possums and provides a wealth of life advice. Pearl and Georgette have been celebrated in a wide range of media, including *New York* magazine's "The Cut," Messy Nessy, BuzzFeed, Jezebel, KQED, The A.V. Club, Oddity Central, and Comedy Central's Tosh.0. Her uncredited videos have appeared on *Good Morning America*, *The Ellen DeGeneres Show*, and *The Late Show with Stephen Colbert*. Pearl's spirit, channeled through Georgette, resides in Astralburg, Etheria.

GEORGETTE SPELVIN IS A LICENSED WILDLIFE REHABILîTATOR specializing in small mammals, who has given hundreds of wildlife workshops and presentations to a variety of audiences from preschoolers to senior citizens. She is married to artist and front man Royce Van Oyster, who capably assists in the operation of her complex animal sanctuary. Georgette worked as a performance artist, professional masseuse, veterinary technician, dual diagnosis counselor in the psychiatric unit of a major metropolitan hospital, and resident storyteller of an international cultural center before her body, mind, and spirit were entirely usurped by a willful little squirrel. Georgette resides with the spirit of Pearl in Astralburg, Etheria.

Acknowledgments

WE ARE ETERNALLY GRATEFUL TO THE FOLLOWING:

Brendan Bigelow for being a technical advisor, social media consultant and all-around great guy and true friend.

Debbie Mitchell of CompanyV for her expert webhosting, graphic design, and for always being on hand to help find the funny.

Anita Camplese, whose camaraderie and willing suspension of disbelief helped to create our world.

And to my beloved Royce Van Oyster, whose multifarious compatible eccentricities and great generosity of spirit make the promise of "ME Pearl in perpetuity" possible.